Ready, Set, Improvise!

Ready, Set, Improvise!

The Nuts and Bolts of Music Improvisation

SUZANNE L. BURTON

ALDEN H. SNELL II

OXFORD
UNIVERSITY PRESS

OXFORD

UNIVERSITY PRESS

Oxford University Press is a department of the University of Oxford. It furthers
the University's objective of excellence in research, scholarship, and education
by publishing worldwide. Oxford is a registered trade mark of Oxford University
Press in the UK and certain other countries.

Published in the United States of America by Oxford University Press
198 Madison Avenue, New York, NY 10016, United States of America.

Library of Congress Cataloging-in-Publication Data
Names: Burton, Suzanne L. author. |
Snell, Alden H., II, author.
Title: Ready, set, improvise! : the nuts and bolts of music improvisation /
Suzanne L. Burton and Alden H. Snell II.
Description: New York, NY : Oxford University Press, [2018] |
Includes bibliographical references.
Identifiers: LCCN 2017054912 | ISBN 9780190675929 (pbk.) |
ISBN 9780190675912 (hardcover) | ISBN 9780190675950 (companion website)
Subjects: LCSH: Improvisation (Music) | Music—Instruction and study.
Classification: LCC MT68.B94 2018 | DDC 781.3/6—dc23
LC record available at https://lccn.loc.gov/2017054912

9 8 7 6 5 4 3 2 1

Paperback printed by WebCom, Inc., Canada
Hardback printed by Bridgeport National Bindery, Inc., United States of America

CONTENTS

ACKNOWLEDGMENTS

THIS BOOK WAS INSPIRED by the expansive research and teaching of Edwin E. Gordon. His legacy has profoundly influenced our teaching practice and scholarship. We also acknowledge the mentors, scholars, and music educators with whom we have had the privilege to work: Christopher Azzara, Beth Bolton, Richard Grunow, Mary Ellen Pinzino, Alison Reynolds, Cynthia Taggart, and Wendy Valerio. We are grateful for their influence on our ever-evolving perspectives on music teaching and learning. Finally, we acknowledge our students, our on-the-ground teachers.

We offer our appreciation to Norm Hirschy and Lauralee Yeary at Oxford University Press, who graciously provided this opportunity for us to expand and codify our pedagogical thinking.

Thank you to John Mills, music engraver extraordinaire, and Kiersten West, who expertly captured our vision for the illustrations.

Finally, a project such as this would not have been possible without the support of our families: Christin, David, Jonathan, and Elizabeth Snell, and Billy and Rachel Burton. Thank you!

ABOUT THE COMPANION WEBSITE

www.oup.com/us/readysetimprovise

Oxford University Press has created a website to accompany *Ready, Set, Improvise! The Nuts and Bolts of Music Improvisation*. The site provides an overview and summary of the book. The reader is encouraged to consult this overview while reading the book.

Ready, Set, Improvise!

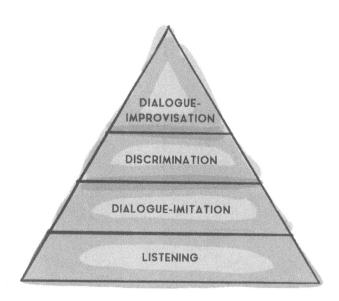

Improvisation Sequence Pyramid

• 1 •

INTRODUCTION

IMPROVISATION IS AN EXCITING part of making music. When improvising, your students synthesize skills and concepts as they spontaneously create unique musical content within a tonal and rhythmic context. Through a sequential approach to improvisation, your students will actively demonstrate musical comprehension by singing, rhythmic chanting, moving, and playing instruments. They will develop as independent musicians, capable of creating music in the moment.

Pedagogical Overview

In this approach, students learn to improvise music in a process that mirrors language development. For example, in language acquisition, children listen, imitate sounds and words, converse, read, and write. Similarly, students listen, perform, improvise, read, and notate music.[1] Just as the listening vocabulary forms the foundation necessary to secure the syntax of language, so it does in music. Students develop a music listening vocabulary by actively audiating, hearing, and participating in music consisting of a variety of tonalities, meters, genres, and styles.

The listening vocabulary provides the springboard for imitating sounds and words in language. In a musical setting, students participate in the first musical interaction, dialogue-imitation. The fundamental skills of listening and imitating build an operational vocabulary for conversation in language. Parallel skills in music form a base for discrimination, the identification of same or different musical ideas, and dialogue-improvisation, in which students create musical content. The ability to improvise leads students to read and notate music with understanding—to audiate what the music will sound like without the aid of a recording or a musical instrument.

A pyramid provides an illustration of how the processes of listening, dialogue-imitation, discrimination, and dialogue-improvisation build on one another for a sequential approach to improvisation. Acquisition and mastery of content, concepts, and skills at each level of the pyramid demonstrate readiness for the next.

Instruction

Whole-part-whole is an instructional strategy through which musical content is presented in its entirety (such as singing an entire song), followed by breaking down the whole into its basic parts (such as tonal or rhythm patterns) with focused practice on those parts, and recombining the parts to form the whole for greater musical understanding. Whole-part-whole is used at each level *within* the pyramid, as well as interactions *among* levels of the pyramid.

Musicianship

To facilitate application of teaching techniques suggested in this book, the following practical skills are recommended:[2]

1. Know a repertoire of songs and chants.
   a. Sing in a variety of tonalities and meters, genres, and styles.
   b. Chant in a variety of meters.

2. Engage in movement.
   a. Emphasize Laban movement efforts of flow, weight, space, and time.[3]
   b. Keep a steady beat.
3. Use tonal and rhythm syllable systems.
   a. Sing with *do*-based major and *la*-based minor solfège.
   b. Chant with rhythm syllables.
4. Create and improvise through singing, chanting, moving, and if applicable, performing on instruments.
5. Read and notate lead sheets for improvisation.

Book Overview

This book presents a sequential process for teaching your students to improvise. Guiding this process are the four levels of the pyramid—listening, dialogue-imitation, discrimination, and dialogue-improvisation, which are addressed in Chapters 2 through 5, respectively.

Repertoire is traced throughout the levels of the pyramid, providing a means for you to track the development of teaching techniques and student learning as you move through the improvisation sequence. In the *Try This!* sections of each chapter, practical ways to implement each process are featured. Additional repertoire is included in the appendix.

Listening, the base of the pyramid and the foundation for all music learning, is presented in Chapter 2. This chapter provides techniques for building students' listening vocabularies. It also includes suggested procedures for teaching songs, chants, and tonal and rhythm patterns, as well as sample activity plans for classroom use.

Chapter 3, Dialogue-Imitation, demonstrates how listening and imitating form the basis for developing a functional vocabulary for improvisation. Repertoire, bass lines, and patterns presented in Chapter 2 are threaded through this process. Solfège and rhythm syllables are introduced to label that which students are audiating, listening to, singing, and chanting. The chapter provides pedagogical techniques for showing students how to imitate rhythm and tonal patterns chanted or sung by the teacher, along with sample imitation activity plans for classroom use.

Dialogue-Imitation is readiness for Discrimination, which is addressed in Chapter 4. When engaged in discrimination, students learn to recognize similarities and differences between tonalities and between meters. In this chapter, we continue to use the repertoire, bass lines, and patterns presented in Chapters 2 and 3. The chapter also provides techniques for teaching students how to discriminate between rhythm patterns in same and different meters and between tonal patterns in same and different tonalities. Sample discrimination activity plans for classroom use are also provided.

When your students can imitate and discriminate between rhythm patterns in different meters and tonal patterns in different tonalities, they are ready to engage in Dialogue-Improvisation, the final level of the pyramid.

Dialogue-Improvisation in music is analogous to conversation in language. When students improvise, they demonstrate comprehension of musical concepts and skills acquired through listening, dialogue-imitation, and discrimination. In Chapter 5, the repertoire, bass lines, and patterns presented in Chapters 2, 3, and 4 continue to be used. Techniques for teaching students to improvise rhythmically, melodically, and harmonically are provided, along with sample improvisation activity plans for classroom use.

The abilities to sing, chant, and move are readiness for playing a musical instrument. Chapter 6, Application to Instruments, provides techniques for improvising on instruments. In this chapter you will find general improvisation techniques that extend the suggestions given in Chapters 2 through 5.

Improvisation is a powerful way to assess music learning. Through assessment, you can monitor the effectiveness of your instruction on student learning. When your students improvise their own rhythms, tonal patterns, and melodies, they are able to create their own music with comprehension. In Chapter 7, assessment techniques that align with each level of the pyramid are shared. Formative assessments for day-to-day instruction; summative assessments to be used several times per year; and techniques for both formative and summative assessment, including checklists, rating scales, and rubrics are offered.

When students are engaged in Listening, Dialogue-Imitation, and Discrimination they learn to synthesize concepts and skills through Dialogue-Improvisation. In this book we provide the nuts and bolts for you to facilitate improvisation with your students. So, get ready, get set, improvise!

• 2 •

LISTENING

JUST AS LISTENING IS the foundation for language learning, music listening is the foundation for music learning. Through active, audiation-based listening, your students will become acculturated to a variety of genres, styles, tonalities, and meters as they are immersed in rich musical content. This chapter presents songs, rhythmic chants, and pedagogical techniques to help you establish listening repertoire for your students from which they will learn to improvise.

Getting Started

Teacher as Musician-Facilitator

Interacting musically with your students is an important part of music learning and teaching; it provides a basis for developing your students' capacity for audiation-based improvisation.[1] Consequently, you are encouraged to facilitate your students' music development by modeling (a) *movement* to foster their embodiment of meter, rhythm, and style; (b) *singing* to anchor tonality, melody, and harmonic functions; and (c) *chanting* to anchor meter, rhythm, and steady beat. Establishing a core listening vocabulary for your students will facilitate musical dialogue when they begin to improvise.

When choosing repertoire, select songs and chants that are of the highest quality and that you are comfortable performing for your students. Perform in keys that your students can easily sing; for example, keys with a tonic of C or D are good for all voice types. Begin with repertoire in major and minor tonalities and duple and triple meters. As you work through the improvisation sequence with your students, enrich their music listening vocabulary with additional songs and chants. When determining the music you will use with your students, choose a diverse repertoire that is short in length, has a simple form, and is representative of various tonalities, meters, genres, and styles. See table 2.1 for one way to organize repertoire with regard to these features.

From time to time, you might wish to use recorded performances for listening activities. Find authentic recordings of music that you are teaching to your class and engage your students in the recommended activities found in this chapter. Continue to develop your students' listening base with recorded selections that are of a variety of genres and styles, making sure that the repertoire and recordings are of high quality.

Repertoire to Sing for Your Students

Presenting a diversified collection of songs to your students is critical for the development of their listening and audiation skills, which are readiness for learning to improvise. The following songs and their bass lines highlight contrasts in melodic, harmonic, and rhythmic content.

Table 2.1 Repertoire Organizer

Title	Composer	Genre	Tonality	Meter	Form
Mozart Sonata Theme	Mozart	Classical	Major	Triple	A A′
Joshua Fit the Battle of Jericho	Unknown	Gospel	Minor	Duple	A A′
Old Joe Clark	Unknown	Folk	Mixolydian	Duple	Chorus-verse
Early to Bed	Benjamin Franklin	Axiom	N/A	Triple	Single phrase
Engine, Engine Number Nine	Traditional	Jump Rope Chant	N/A	Duple	A A′
Dessert	Suzanne Burton	Chant	N/A	Asymmetrical (in 7)	Single phrase

Note: Additional suggestions for common, public domain repertoire may be found in the appendix.

Figure 2.1. Theme from Mozart's Piano Sonata in A (K. 331)

Figure 2.2. Bass line from Mozart's Piano Sonata in A (K. 331)

The theme from Mozart's Piano Sonata in A (K. 331) is a beautiful, lyrical melody in major tonality and triple meter (see figure 2.1). This theme, which is presented with its corresponding bass line (figure 2.2), has a simple harmonic progression of tonic and dominant chord functions. Bass lines provide students with a harmonic context from which to understand harmonic patterns and prepare students to improvise with an understanding of tonality and harmonic progression.

In contrast to the Mozart example, "Joshua Fit the Battle of Jericho" is a spiritual in minor tonality with a duple meter swinging style (see figure 2.3). Underpinning this song is a bass line that comprises tonic and dominant functions (see figure 2.4).

Whole-Part-Whole Techniques for Singing

Developing a foundation for listening by immersing your students in music is the goal of the first level of the pyramid. Using a *whole-part-whole* approach when performing songs for your students will help them develop such a foundation.[2]

Before singing the Mozart Sonata Theme or "Joshua Fit the Battle of Jericho" and their bass lines to your students, sing a *tune-up* (see figures 2.5, 2.6, 2.7, and 2.8) that is in the same tonality and meter as the song. The tune-up will prepare students' audiation for the song that is to come. Pause momentarily. Then, keeping whole-part-whole instruction in mind, begin the

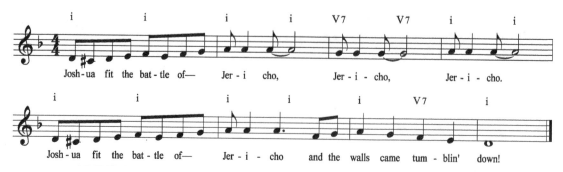

Figure 2.3. Melody of "Joshua Fit the Battle of Jericho"

Figure 2.4. Bass line for "Joshua Fit the Battle of Jericho"

A note on performing melodic and harmonic patterns for your students:

Melodic patterns are a combination of pitch and rhythm and should be performed in the tempo, meter, and style of the piece you are teaching. Harmonic patterns should be sung without rhythm in order to focus your students' attention on the harmonic functions and tonality of the song. To encourage students to audiate, pause and breathe between each pattern you sing.

first *whole* by singing the song and its bass line on neutral syllables. Be consistent with each performance, singing the song in the same key, tonality, and meter each time.

Next break the song into *parts,* which may include the tonic, to assist students with audiating a sense of "home," melodic patterns (see figures 2.9 and 2.10) to feature the characteristic tones and meter of the repertoire, or harmonic patterns (see figures 2.11 and 2.12) to draw attention to the way the chords function in the song.[3] From class to class, vary the part by singing the tonic, bass line, melodic pattern, or harmonic pattern in the same key as the song. Take care to expose your students to all four parts in a systematic way.

After singing the part for your students, perform the whole again—the complete song and bass line—with expression and a sense of style. As you sing these melodies and bass lines on neutral syllables to your students, they will become familiar with the themes and acculturated to the tonality, meter, harmonic progression, and style of each piece. If a song has words, you may wish to include them every so often.

Figure 2.5. Major tonality duple meter tune-up

Figure 2.6. Major tonality triple meter tune-up

Figure 2.7. Minor tonality duple meter tune-up

Figure 2.8. Minor tonality triple meter tune-up

Figure 2.9. Melodic patterns for the theme from Mozart's Piano Sonata in A (K. 331)

Figure 2.10. Melodic patterns for "Joshua Fit the Battle of Jericho"

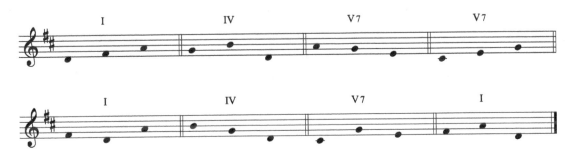

Figure 2.11. Major tonality harmonic patterns

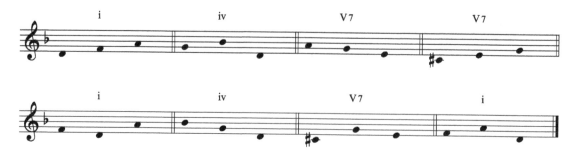

Figure 2.12.   Minor tonality harmonic patterns

In the following "Try This!" activity, students are immersed in the song "Joshua Fit the Battle of Jericho." This activity may be used in instrumental or general music settings.

Try This!
Harmonic Pattern Immersion Activity

FOCUS

Immersing students in a harmonic minor tonality and duple meter song that has a swing style

PREPARE

"Joshua Fit the Battle of Jericho"
Harmonic minor patterns
5 to 7 minutes of class time

ANIMATE

Sing the minor tonality, duple meter tune-up to "Joshua Fit the Battle of Jericho" on neutral syllables. Begin moving to the macrobeat (primary beat), tapping hands on thighs in bilateral motion. Invite students to move with you. Then, while moving, sing the song, varying the place on your body where you tap the macrobeat. At the end of the song, have students freeze in place while you sing harmonic patterns between repetitions. End the activity with a repetition of the song and its bass line. Be playful and experiment with expression and style!

ASSESS

No formal assessment is necessary when engaging students in developing the listening vocabulary in this activity.

Repertoire to Chant for Your Students

"Early to Bed," presented in figure 2.13, is a triple meter chant with a text based on the well-known axiom attributed to Benjamin Franklin. Notice that the rhythm is simple, comprising macrobeats (primary beats) and microbeats (secondary beats), which will anchor your students' audiation in triple meter.

In contrast to "Early to Bed," the well-known American jump rope chant "Engine, Engine Number Nine" is in duple meter. This chant, presented in figure 2.14, also has a strong emphasis on rhythm anchors of macrobeats and microbeats.

Before presenting a chant for your students, establish meter by performing a tune-up of macrobeats and microbeats in the meter and tempo of the chant (see figures 2.15 and 2.16). Then, proceed with the whole-part-whole technique of presenting the chant.

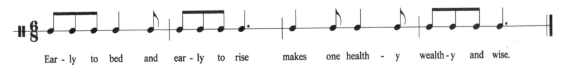

Figure 2.13. "Early to Bed"

Figure 2.14. "Engine, Engine, Number nine"

Figure 2.15. Triple meter tune-up

Figure 2.16. Duple meter tune-up

Figure 2.17. Triple meter rhythm patterns

Figure 2.18. Duple meter rhythm patterns

Rhythm patterns should be performed in the meter and tempo of the piece. Chants should be performed on one pitch with inflection to focus your students' attention on the rhythmic aspect of the music without being distracted by elements of pitch and tonality. Invite students to move with you, in flow, and to macrobeats and microbeats in time. To encourage students' audiation, breathe in time between each rhythm pattern you chant.

A note on neutral syllables:
At first, students need to hear and audiate music without being encumbered by text or labels; thus we recommend primarily using neutral syllables (such as "oo," "bah," or "bum") as you sing or chant to your students.

Whole-Part-Whole Techniques for Chanting

For the first whole, perform the chant in its entirety, being expressive, adding inflection to your performance without using your singing voice. Perform the chant on neutral syllables so that students are saturated in the music, rather than the text. Be consistent with each performance, chanting in the same meter and tempo each time. Consider moving with flowing and fluid movement, inviting students to move with you. This will facilitate students' listening to, feeling for, and audiation of the rhythm and meter without the imposition of beat.

To introduce students to steady beat, move to the macrobeat with your heels and to the microbeat by bilaterally patting your thighs.[4] For the part, perform four-macrobeat-long rhythm patterns in the meter and tempo of that chant (see figures 2.17 and 2.18 for examples of rhythm patterns). Finally, perform the whole chant again. If a chant has words, every so often you may wish to perform it with the text. Your students will have a deeper understanding of the repertoire you are presenting when you follow this model.

In the following "Try This!" activity, students are immersed in a triple meter chant. Use this activity in instrumental or general music settings.

Try This!
Rhythm Immersion Activity

FOCUS

Immersing students in a triple meter chant

PREPARE

"Early to Bed"
Large stretchy band
7 to 10 minutes of class time

ANIMATE

Invite students to sit or stand in a circle on the floor and grasp a section of the stretchy band. Chant the triple meter tune-up to establish the meter. Begin performing "Early to Bed" on neutral syllables while you and your students move the therapy band forward and backward in a rocking motion on the macrobeat. Every so often intersperse triple meter rhythm patterns between repetitions. End the activity with a repetition of "Early to Bed."

ASSESS

No formal assessment is necessary when engaging students in developing the listening vocabulary in this activity.

Enriching Your Students' Listening Vocabulary

Many songs and chants are outside major and minor tonalities and duple and triple meters. Varying the tonalities and meters of the repertoire you present for your students will enrich and expand their listening vocabulary. Providing students with a variety of content allows them to make musical comparisons. Two examples of this principle follow. Additional songs and chants in a variety of tonalities and meters may be found in the appendix.

In mixolydian tonality and duple meter, "Old Joe Clark" is a popular folk song presented in figure 2.19. The straight microbeat feel of the verse, coupled with the jaunty chorus, makes this a song that your students will enjoy listening and moving to.

Figure 2.19. Melody of "Old Joe Clark"

Figure 2.20. "Dessert"

"Dessert" is a fun chant in asymmetrical meter (see figure 2.20). The emphasis on microbeats (eighth notes) at the beginning of the chant followed by macrobeats (quarter and dotted quarter notes) reinforces the uniqueness of asymmetrical meter.

Music learning continuously returns to listening. As students listen to you sing and chant repertoire in a variety of tonalities and meters, they will naturally desire to respond musically. A robust listening vocabulary provides readiness and a foundation for instruction at the next level of the pyramid, Dialogue-Imitation.

• 3 •

DIALOGUE-IMITATION

THE FUNDAMENTAL SKILLS OF listening and imitating form the
basis on which students develop a functional vocabulary for improvisation. Like language, we begin speaking by imitating sounds that eventually coalesce into words and sentences, we begin by making musical
sounds through imitation. In Dialogue-Imitation, students formally
learn to sing songs and perform chants, as well as exercise their listening vocabulary by imitating melodic and harmonic patterns sung by
the teacher and rhythm patterns chanted by the teacher. In this chapter,
repertoire and patterns from Chapter 2 are woven throughout in a
whole-part-whole approach to (a) reinforce the sequential connection
between the listening vocabulary and Dialogue-Imitation, providing
a foundation for Discrimination; (b) facilitate the use of solfège and
rhythm syllables to label what is audiated, heard, sung, or chanted; and
(c) demonstrate pedagogical techniques for and rhythm imitation activities. As you continue the improvisation sequence with your students,
be sure to introduce new repertoire in the Listening process. Doing so
will build students' listening vocabularies, deepening their foundation
for future improvisation.

Whole-Part-Whole Techniques for Singing

In Dialogue-Imitation, students learn to sing the melodies and bass
lines you have previously performed in the Listening process. The

following procedure provides opportunities for students to listen to a song and its bass line (*whole*); be immersed in its tonality and meter; audiate and sing the tonic or melodic or harmonic patterns (*part*); and learn to sing the song, with greater understanding of the tonal aspects that are the basis for the song (*whole*).

Whole-Part-Whole Lesson Plan 3.1

Whole-Part-Whole Procedures: Singing on Neutral Syllables

WHOLE

- Sing the tune-up on neutral syllables to establish the tonality and meter of the song for your students.
- Sing the song and its bass line on neutral syllables.

PART

- Sing the tonic on a neutral syllable for students. Invite students to audiate the tonic.
- Sing the tonic for students, then sing the song and its bass line. Stop at musical intervals such as phrase endings. At these points, sing the tonic for students, then gesture for them to breathe and sing the tonic in imitation.

PART (VARIATION I)

- Sing melodic patterns from Chapter 2 on a neutral syllable for students. Invite students to imitate the patterns. Continue teaching each pattern in the sequence.
- Sing the song and then the bass line. Stop at musical intervals such as phrase endings. At each point, sing a melodic pattern for students, then gesture for them to breathe and sing the melodic pattern in imitation. Invite the class or individual students to sing solo. Continue teaching each pattern in the sequence.

PART (VARIATION II)

- Sing harmonic patterns on a neutral syllable for students. Invite them to imitate the harmonic patterns. Continue teaching each pattern in the sequence.
- Sing the song and then the bass line. Stop at musical intervals such as phrase endings. At each pause, sing a harmonic pattern for students, then gesture for them to breathe and sing the harmonic pattern in imitation. Invite the class or individual students to sing. Continue teaching each pattern in the sequence.

PART (VARIATION III)

- After students have learned the melody and bass line, invite them to sing the melody on neutral syllables while you sing the bass line.
- Invite students to sing the bass line while you sing the melody.
- Divide the class into two groups. Ask one group to sing the melody and the other the bass line. Then, have the groups switch parts.

PART (VARIATION IV)

- Sing the tune-up in the tonality and meter of the song. Invite students to audiate the song and raise their hands when done.

WHOLE

- Sing the tune-up in the tonality and meter of the song. Invite students to sing the song.

EXTEND

- Teach students the words to the song.
- If necessary, re-teach parts of the song and bass line.

From one class to another, vary the repertoire and the *part* so that students learn how to audiate and sing the tonic of the song, characteristic tones of the melody, and harmonic functions associated with the song. For the first class period, teach the Mozart Sonata Theme and corresponding major melodic patterns. In the next class, teach "Joshua Fit the Battle of Jericho" and corresponding harmonic minor melodic patterns. Follow this procedure with the same repertoire, but this time switch to harmonic patterns. To further emphasize the harmonic progression of a song, follow the steps for combining a song and its bass line for harmonic accompaniment.

From Neutral Syllables to Solfège

When approximately 80 percent of your class can imitate the tonic and the melodic and harmonic patterns on neutral syllables, begin to introduce solfège. Solfège will assist your students with audiating what they sing. It will also help your students identify tonality, bass lines, and harmonic functions. For solfège, a system based on moveable *do*, in which *do* will match the key signature of the music, is recommended. In other words, if the key signature contains three sharps, A is *do*. If the key signature has one flat, F is *do*, and so on. Songs in major tonality have a tonic of *do*, and minor songs rest on *la*. The tonic of dorian is *re*; phrygian, *mi*; lydian, *fa*; mixolydian, *so*; and locrian, *ti*. Representative of tonal relationships, solfège should always be sung and not spoken. Adapting the whole-part-whole approach of neutral syllables to solfège is simple: Continue singing the song on neutral syllables, but now perform the tune-up and the tonic, melodic, and harmonic patterns on solfège.

Whole-Part-Whole Lesson Plan 3.2

Whole-Part-Whole Procedures: Singing with Solfège

WHOLE

- Sing the tune-up on *solfège* to establish the tonality and meter of the song for your students.
- Sing the song on *neutral* syllables and the bass line on *solfège*.

PART

- Sing the tonic on *solfège* for students. Invite students to audiate the tonic.
- Sing the tonic for students, then sing the song and the bass line on neutral syllables. Stop at musical intervals such as phrase endings. At these points, sing the tonic for students, then gesture for them to breathe and sing the tonic in imitation. Invite the class or individual students to sing.
- Identify the tonality of the song based on audiation of the tonic. If the tonic is *do*, the tonality is major. If the tonic is *la*, the tonality is minor.

PART (VARIATION I)

- Sing melodic patterns on *solfège* for students. Invite the class or individual students to imitate the melodic patterns.
- Sing the song and bass line. Stop at musical intervals such as phrase endings. At these points, sing melodic patterns for students, then gesture for them to breathe and sing melodic patterns in imitation. Invite the class or individual students to sing.

PART (VARIATION II)

- Sing harmonic patterns on *solfège* for students. Invite the class or individual students to sing the patterns for you in imitation.
- Teach students to identify harmonic patterns and their functions.
- Sing the song and the bass line. Stop at musical intervals such as phrase endings. At these points, sing harmonic patterns for students, then gesture for them to breathe and sing the harmonic patterns in imitation. Invite the class or individual students to sing.
- Sing the song and the bass line. Stop at musical intervals such as phrase endings. At these points, sing harmonic patterns for students, then gesture for students to breathe and name the harmonic function. Invite the class or individual students to respond with the labels.

PART (VARIATION III)

- Sing the tune-up in the tonality and meter of the song on *solfège*. Invite students to audiate the song and raise their hands when done.

WHOLE

- Sing the tune-up in the tonality and meter of the song. Invite students to sing the song.

EXTEND

- Teach students the words to the song.
- If necessary, re-teach parts of the song and the bass line.

Techniques for Teaching Melodic and Harmonic Patterns

Melodic Patterns

Melodic patterns focus on the characteristic tones of a tonality and ultimately prepare students for melodic improvisation. These patterns tend to be easier than harmonic patterns for students to imitate and so should be taught first. When teaching melodic patterns, sing them in rhythm and meter, and in the style of the music. With each pattern, breathe before singing it for your students, then gesture for them to take a breath and sing the pattern in imitation.

Repeat the sequence of instruction several times, moving from the song to melodic patterns and back to the song. In this way, students will audiate the characteristic tones within the tonality of the song. As students become comfortable singing in imitation as a group, invite individual students to sing solo.

Harmonic Patterns

Harmonic patterns emphasize the underlying harmonic progression of the tonality of a song. When teaching harmonic patterns to students, sing them without rhythm or meter, with each pitch slightly separated. As with melodic patterns, breathe before singing the pattern, then gesture to students to take a breath and sing the pattern in imitation. Repeat the sequence of instruction several times, moving from the song to harmonic patterns and back to the song. Continue to build students' comfort levels with singing and invite them to perform individually for you.

Labeling Harmonic Functions

Being able to identify harmonic functions will help your students improvise accompaniments to songs they are familiar with. As your students become comfortable imitating harmonic patterns on solfège begin to teach them how to label the harmonic functions. Continuing with the whole-part-whole approach, sing the tune-up to set the context (whole). Ask students to sing the song. Then, teach your students how to label tonality and the functions of the harmonic patterns in that tonality (part). For example, in major tonality, tonic patterns are a combination of *do-mi-so*, subdominant *fa-la-do*, and dominant *so-ti-re-fa*. In minor tonality, tonic patterns are a combination of is *la-do-mi*, subdominant is *re-fa-la*, and dominant is *mi-si-ti-re*. When teaching how to label harmonic patterns, your students first sing the song and bass line for context. Then they imitate your model of singing and labeling harmonic patterns in the key of the song. Sing the functions on the root of each chord. After several repetitions of function identification, finish the activity with singing the song (whole).

In the following activity, students imitate melodic patterns that you sing on solfège. They also learn to use solfège to label tonality.

Try This!
Major Tonality Melodic Pattern Imitation

FOCUS

Introducing solfège to label pitch and tonality through imitation

PREPARE

Mozart Sonata Theme
Major tonality melodic patterns
Ball
7 to 10 minutes of class time

ANIMATE

Ask students to sit in a circle on the floor. Invite them to sing the Mozart Sonata Theme on neutral syllables and the bass line on solfège. At the end of the song, sing a melodic pattern on solfège. Then, roll a ball to an individual student, which signifies the student should imitate that pattern. Continue this process as you cycle through the sequence of melodic patterns. Then, perform the song again. Remind the students that when *do* is the tonic the tonality is major, and *la* is the tonic for minor. Identify the tonality of the melody with the class. Repeat the activity several times, ending with a final repetition of the song.

ASSESS

Students will be assessed with regard to their ability to individually imitate melodic patterns on solfège with accuracy.

Whole-Part-Whole Techniques for Chanting

In Dialogue-Imitation, your students are invited to learn the chants you have previously performed for them. The following procedure provides opportunities for students to listen to a chant (whole), audiate rhythm and meter and perform rhythm patterns (part), and return to the chant (whole).

Whole-Part-Whole Lesson Plan 3.3
Whole-Part-Whole Procedures: Chanting on Neutral Syllables

WHOLE

- Perform a tune-up on neutral syllables in the meter of the chant.
- Perform the chant on neutral syllables for students.

PART

- While you perform the chant, invite students to follow your model and
  - move to the macrobeat with their heels.
  - move to the microbeat with hands patting their thighs.
  - move to the macrobeat and microbeat together.

PART (VARIATION I)

- While you perform the chant, invite students to follow your model and
  - move to the macrobeat while chanting neutral syllables on the macrobeat.
  - move to the microbeat while chanting neutral syllables on the microbeat.

PART (VARIATION II)

- Perform a tune-up on neutral syllables to set the context of the chant. Perform the chant and stop at musical points to give the class or individual students four-macrobeat rhythm patterns on neutral syllables. Invite students to imitate your rhythm patterns as a class or individually.

PART (VARIATION III)

- Perform the tune-up in the meter of the chant. Invite students to audiate the chant and raise their hands when done.

WHOLE

- Perform the tune-up in the meter of the chant. Invite students to perform the chant on neutral syllables.

EXPAND

- Teach students the words to the chant.
- Re-teach parts of the chant as needed.

From Neutral Syllables to Rhythm Syllables

Rhythm syllables will help your students audiate and feel macrobeats and microbeats and identify meter. For rhythm syllables we recommend a system based on beat function whereby, instead of labeling notes based on notation, rhythm and meter are labeled on the basis of how they are audiated, felt, and grouped.[1] The syllable *du* is audiated and chanted as the macrobeat. The microbeats for duple meter are audiated and chanted as *du-de*, and for triple meter, *du-da-di*. Divisions of duple meter are audiated as *du-ta-de-ta*, whereas they are *du-ta-da-ta-di-ta* in triple meter. When in asymmetrical meter, the macrobeats continue to be labeled as *du*; the microbeats are *du-be* for groupings of two and *du-ba-bi* for groupings of three.[2]

Whole-Part-Whole Lesson Plan 3.4

Whole-Part-Whole Procedures: Chanting with Rhythm Syllables

WHOLE

- Perform a tune-up on *rhythm* syllables in the meter of the chant.
- Perform the chant for students on *neutral* syllables.

PART

- While you perform the chant, invite students to follow your model and
  - move to the macrobeat while chanting rhythm syllables.
  - move to the microbeat while chanting rhythm syllables.
- Identify the meter through the audiation and labeling of microbeats and macrobeats.

PART (VARIATION I)

- Perform a tune-up on rhythm syllables to set the context of the chant.
- Perform the chant and stop at musical points to give the class or individual students four-macrobeat rhythm patterns on rhythm syllables. Invite students to imitate your rhythm patterns as a class or individually.

PART (VARIATION II)

- Perform the tune-up in the meter of the chant. Invite students to audiate the chant and raise their hands when done.

WHOLE

- Perform the tune-up in the meter of the chant. Invite students to perform the chant on neutral syllables.

EXPAND

- Teach students the words to the chant.

Techniques for Teaching Rhythm Patterns

Rhythm patterns focus on the audiation of meter, rhythm, and melodic rhythm. They are always chanted in meter and time. They ultimately prepare students for both rhythmic and melodic improvisation. When teaching rhythm patterns, begin with a tune-up and a chant in the same meter as the rhythm patterns. Using the suggested four-macrobeat patterns, comprising rhythm anchors of macrobeats and microbeats, perform the patterns in time and in the meter of the rhythmic chant they are associated with. As you perform a pattern for your students to imitate, gesture to them to breathe on the third macrobeat of the pattern. The breath will facilitate their audiation and aid with keeping the imitative dialogue between you and your students in time, meter, and tempo. Return to the chant. Repeat the instructional approach of whole-part-whole with the chant and associated rhythm patterns. Just as you would with songs, vary the chant repertoire and the part so that your students continue to learn how to audiate a wide variety of meters and rhythms.

Imitation of duple meter patterns on rhythm syllables is the focus of the following lesson plan. Your students will learn how to perform duple meter macrobeat and microbeat ostinati to a previously learned chant.

Try This!
Duple Meter Pattern Imitation

FOCUS

Moving to macrobeat and microbeats while chanting macrobeat and microbeat ostinati on rhythm syllables

PREPARE

"Engine, Engine Number Nine"
Egg shakers
7 to 10 minutes of class time

ANIMATE

Invite students to stand, spreading out in the classroom and standing in self-space. As you perform the chant, ask students to pulse the macrobeat and chant *du*. Next, invite students to move to the microbeat while chanting *du-de*. Pass out one egg shaker per student. Divide the class. While you perform the chant, have one group pulse the egg shakers while chanting the macrobeat, *du*, and the other group pulse the microbeat while chanting *du-de*. In between repetitions of the chant, perform four-macrobeat rhythm patterns on rhythm syllables, inviting the group or individuals to imitate your patterns. Resume the activity, having students switch parts of the ostinato. Eventually, ask students to audiate the rhythm syllables and no longer chant them.

ASSESS

Students will be assessed with regard to their ability to individually imitate rhythm patterns on rhythm syllables with accuracy.

Enriching Your Students' Listening Vocabulary

Continue to teach your students songs and chants in an array of tonalities and meters. The song "Old Joe Clark" and the chant "Dessert" are both good examples of the type of repertoire that stimulates audiation of many types, forms, and styles of music. Exposing your students to songs and chants in a variety of tonalities and meters will expand your students' listening vocabulary, forming a broad base of repertoire from which to glean musical ideas.

When teaching melodic, harmonic, or rhythm patterns, invite students to respond individually. This affords the opportunity for individualized assessment (see Chapter 7 for assessment strategies) and for you to learn whether they are imitating your patterns accurately. When approximately 80 percent of your students accurately imitate melodic and harmonic patterns on solfège and rhythm patterns on rhythm syllables, begin to engage them in Discrimination activities, by which they learn to compare similarities and differences in music.

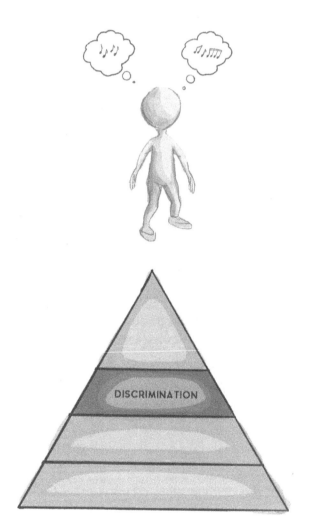

• 4 •

DISCRIMINATION

DISCRIMINATION IS A SKILL that your students will use to recognize similarities and differences between and among tonalities and meters through comparison.[1] In language children learn differences between words and sentences; in Discrimination, students learn how to identify and describe *same* and *different* musical content. In this chapter, musical content is based on the focus repertoire of the book: the Mozart Sonata Theme, "Joshua Fit the Battle of Jericho," "Early to Bed," and "Engine, Engine Number Nine," which are woven throughout the improvisation sequence. This repertoire brings context to the melodic, harmonic, and rhythm patterns that students audiate, imitate, and discriminate—all of which provide readiness for improvisation. In this chapter, Discrimination activities follow from the Listening and Dialogue-Imitation processes and are presented through (a) solfège and rhythm syllables that are used to identify, label, and describe same and different aspects of music; (b) a whole-part-whole approach; and (c) specific techniques for teaching melodic, harmonic, and rhythmic discrimination. As your students become comfortable identifying *same* and *different*, they learn to discriminate, eventually becoming able to create something new.

Whole-Part-Whole Approach

Begin melodic, harmonic, or rhythm discrimination by establishing the tonal or rhythmic context with a song or chant that is familiar to your students. Use repertoire as the first *whole* and invite your students to sing the song and bass line or perform the chant. Then, proceed with discrimination activities that emphasize the melodic, harmonic, and rhythmic *parts* of the music. End the activity with the final *whole,* a repetition of the song or chant that was used to establish tonal or rhythmic context.

Melodic Discrimination

Comparing Melodic Patterns

Students first compare melodic patterns that are in the same tonality and are representative of the repertoire they are learning in melodic discrimination. Establish major or minor tonality with a song in that tonality. Tell students that you will sing two patterns and they are to decide if the melody of the patterns is the same or different. Sing the patterns in the style and tempo of the music on neutral syllables for the students. To indicate which pattern you are presenting, hold up one finger when singing the first. Pause momentarily for a breath and hold up two fingers when performing the second. After you have sung both patterns, ask students to indicate whether they were the same or different. One technique is to use hand signals. Ask students to hold out two closed fists in front of them for patterns they are audiating as the same. If they are audiating patterns as different, have students hold out one closed fist and an open hand. Ask students why they audiated the patterns as the same or different and have them respond using solfège to label the pitches of the patterns they heard you sing. Teach melodic patterns in both major and minor tonalities. Figures 4.1 and 4.2 present examples based on the Mozart Sonata Theme and "Joshua Fit the Battle of Jericho," respectively.

Comparing Pairs of Melodic Patterns in One Tonality

When your class confidently identifies individual patterns as same or different, sing pairs of melodic patterns in order to develop students' readiness to discriminate between musical phrases. Set the tonal context, then present pairs of melodic patterns (see figures 4.3 and 4.4) with the

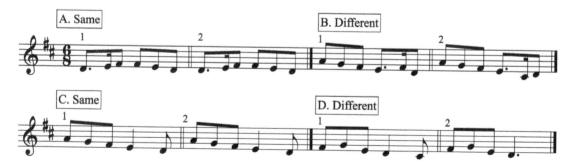

Figure 4.1. Major melodic discrimination patterns

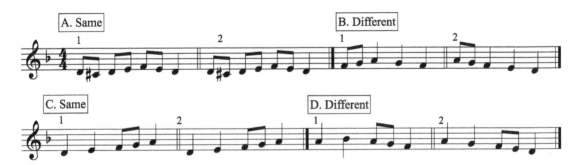

Figure 4.2. Minor melodic discrimination patterns

Figure 4.3. Pairs of major melodic discrimination patterns

same technique you used before. Invite students to demonstrate with hand signals whether they are audiating the same or different pairs of patterns. Have them support their choice of same or different by singing on solfège the pitches they were audiating for each pattern.

After students have achieved competency discriminating between pairs of patterns in major and minor tonalities, invite them to compare melodic phrases.

Comparing Melodic Phrases in One Tonality

To further expand melodic content, perform complete phrases and ask your students to discriminate between them. Combine pairs of patterns into phrases, based on content from either

Figure 4.4.   Pairs of minor melodic discrimination patterns

figure 4.3 or figure 4.4, and ask students to demonstrate whether they are audiating same or different phrases. For instance, after setting a major tonal context, sing the A patterns from figure 4.3. Then, either repeat the same patterns from line A or sing patterns from line B for the second phrase. Ask students to demonstrate whether the phrases were the same or different and ask them why they made that choice (for instance, What tonality were you audiating for these phrases? What is the tonic of that tonality?). Whenever possible, have them use solfège to support their answers. Repeat this process in minor tonality.

Comparing Melodic Patterns in Different Tonalities

As your students gain skill in comparing melodic patterns and phrases in one tonality, ask them to discriminate between melodic patterns and phrases that are in different tonalities. Figures 4.5 and 4.6 present two examples based on the repertoire students are learning. Related to the Mozart Sonata Theme is one pair of patterns in major tonality followed by the same pair in parallel minor, both in triple meter. Representative of "Joshua Fit the Battle of Jericho," figure 4.6 presents a pair of patterns in minor tonality followed by the same pair in parallel major, both in duple meter. In this case, do not set a tonal context for students when comparing tonalities.

Figure 4.5. Melodic patterns in major and minor tonalities

Figure 4.6. Melodic patterns in minor and major tonalities

Instead, on neutral syllables, perform example 1 followed by example 2, using the same teaching techniques as before. Question students regarding the tonality of each set of patterns and invite them to sing, on solfège, the tonic and the pitches of the patterns that guided their thinking.

Comparing Melodic Phrases in Different Tonalities

To compare melodic phrases in different tonalities, follow a process similar to the one you used with melodic patterns in different tonalities. Drawing from the repertoire students are learning, sing two phrases on neutral syllables, but in different tonalities. You might sing the first phrase of "Joshua Fit the Battle of Jericho" in minor tonality and repeat the same phrase in major tonality. Or, sing the first phrase in major tonality and repeat the phrase in the original minor tonality.

Remember to repeat phrases in the same tonality to prevent students from assuming that you will always change tonality. Ask students to compare the two phrases and identify them as the same or different and to then identify the tonality they were audiating for each phrase.

Harmonic Discrimination

As they engage in discrimination, your students' understanding of harmonic functions will expand. Discriminating between harmonic patterns will assist them with audiating the harmonic underpinnings of music.

Comparing Harmonic Patterns in One Function

To prepare students for discriminating between harmonic patterns in one function, first review the harmonic patterns presented in Chapter 2 (see figures 2.11 and 2.12). Invite your students to sing the patterns with solfège and to identify the patterns' functions. Next, tell students that you will sing two major tonic patterns on neutral syllables and you would like them to identify whether the patterns are the same or different. Follow the same procedure you used to teach melodic pattern discrimination. After students indicate whether they audiated the patterns you sang as same or different, ask them how they arrived at their answers: What pitches were you audiating for the first pattern? The second? In what chord function are these patterns? Continue teaching tonic function patterns in both tonalities (see figures 4.7 and 4.8) and expand the activity to dominant-seventh and subdominant functions.

Comparing Harmonic Functions within One Tonality

As your students develop competency with discriminating between patterns in one function, invite them to make comparisons among functions within one tonality. With the harmonic patterns from Chapter 2 (see also figures 4.9 and 4.10), establish a tonal context of major or minor. Inform your students that you will sing two harmonic function patterns in that tonality and that they are to determine whether the patterns are the same or different. Sing a set of two patterns. Ask the students to indicate whether the two patterns were the same or different. Question students about their answers; ask what chord functions they were audiating and have

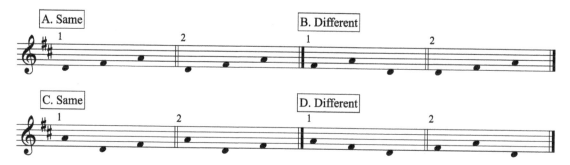

Figure 4.7. Same and different major tonic patterns

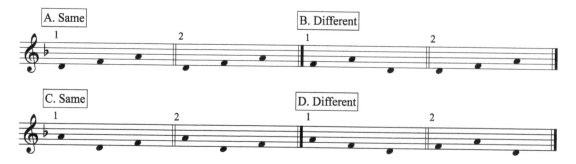

Figure 4.8. Same and different minor tonic patterns

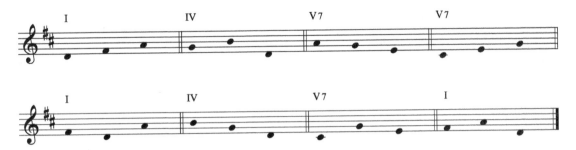

Figure 4.9. Major tonality harmonic patterns

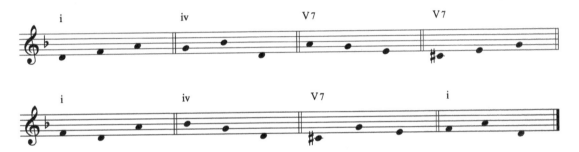

Figure 4.10. Minor tonality harmonic patterns

them use solfège to demonstrate how they arrived at their answers. Gradually increase the number of patterns to sets of three or four harmonic patterns.

Comparing Tonalities with Harmonic Patterns

When students are comfortable identifying similarities and differences between individual patterns within one function and patterns between several functions, invite them to discriminate between different tonalities.

Begin with the major and minor harmonic patterns from figures 4.9 and 4.10. Inform students that you are going to sing two series of harmonic patterns on neutral syllables and that they are to compare the patterns to determine the tonality of each series. As an example, sing the first three major patterns given in figure 4.9, ending with a tonic pattern. Holding up one finger, perform this series of patterns. Then, after taking a breath, hold up two fingers and either repeat that same series of patterns or perform the series in parallel minor (see figure 4.10). Ask students to identify whether

Perform all patterns on neutral syllables to optimize audiation. Have students use labeling skills to identify similarities and differences between and among patterns and the music.

the series are the same or different, and encourage them to use solfège when answering questions about the tonality and functions they are audiating. Continue using patterns from figures 4.9 and 4.10 to outline major and minor tonalities. Eventually, create your own patterns for this activity.

The following activity emphasizes harmonic function patterns in minor tonality. Students determine whether the patterns are the same or different and label those patterns using their solfège skills to demonstrate their understanding.

Try This!
Discrimination of Harmonic Functions

FOCUS

Comparing harmonic functions within one tonality

PREPARE

Mozart Sonata Theme
Hula Hoops
Major harmonic function patterns
7 to 10 minutes of class time

ANIMATE

Place Hula Hoops around the classroom space. Ask students to find a hoop and stand in it. As you begin singing the Mozart Sonata Theme, invite students to move about the room. At the end of the song, sing two major harmonic function patterns on neutral syllables. If the patterns are the same, students stand outside of the hoop they are nearest. If different, they step inside the closest hoop. Ask individual students questions such as why they chose same or different as their answer and what pitches and harmonic functions they were audiating. Have students justify their answers by singing their responses on solfège.

ASSESS

Students will be informally assessed regarding their comprehension of same or different harmonic functions and the labeling of those functions.

Rhythm Discrimination

Comparing Rhythm Patterns in One Meter

Begin teaching rhythm discrimination by setting a rhythmic context with a chant in triple or duple meter such as or "Early to Bed" or "Engine, Engine Number Nine." Then, tell your students that you will chant one rhythm pattern followed by another in the same meter and that they are to decide if they are auditing the two patterns as the same or different. (See figures 4.11 and 4.12 for examples of triple and duple meter patterns.) Next, perform the first pattern while holding up one finger. Chant the pattern, pause briefly to breathe in meter and time, and hold up two fingers when performing the second pattern. Ask students to indicate whether the patterns were the same or different and to chant the syllables they were auditing for each pattern. Use neutral syllables when performing the patterns and chant both patterns in the same tempo.

Comparing Pairs of Rhythm Patterns in One Meter

As students become comfortable discriminating between individual rhythm patterns, extend the process and invite students to compare pairs of rhythm patterns. Figures 4.13 and 4.14

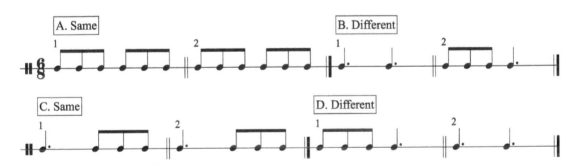

Figure 4.11. Triple meter discrimination patterns

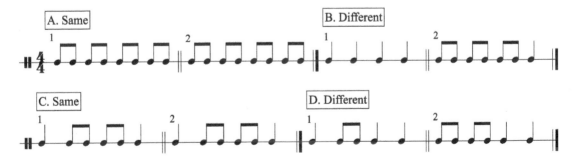

Figure 4.12. Duple meter discrimination patterns

Figure 4.13. Pairs of triple meter discrimination patterns

Figure 4.14. Pairs of duple meter discrimination patterns

present examples for your use. Follow the process for teaching discrimination of individual patterns, performing the patterns on neutral syllables. Have students show whether they were audiating the patterns as the same or different, and ask them to chant rhythm syllables and move to the macrobeat and the microbeat to demonstrate their answers.

When students confidently discriminate between pairs of patterns in one meter, begin presenting rhythmic phrases for students to compare.

Comparing Rhythmic Phrases in One Meter

To expand rhythmic content, compare rhythmic phrases in one meter. Create phrases by combining pairs of patterns from figure 4.13 or figure 4.14 and invite students to demonstrate whether they are audiating the same or different rhythmic phrases. For example, set a duple or triple meter rhythmic context and perform patterns from line A and line B of the corresponding meter. Ask students to indicate if they were audiating the phrases as the same or different. Ask them about the meter they were audiating, and have them use rhythm syllables and movement when defining their answers.

Comparing Rhythm Patterns in Different Meters

Invite your students to discriminate between patterns in more than one meter. In figure 4.15 a pair of patterns in triple meter is followed by a similar pair in duple meter. In figure 4.16 a pair of patterns in duple meter is followed by a pair of triple meter patterns. Do not establish meter. Instead, using neutral syllables, perform one pair of patterns, pause, and perform the other pair. Ask students to indicate whether they were audiating the same or different phrases and to identify the meter of each pair through audiation. Have them justify their answers by chanting the rhythm syllables of those patterns.

Figure 4.15. Pairs of rhythm patterns in triple and duple meters

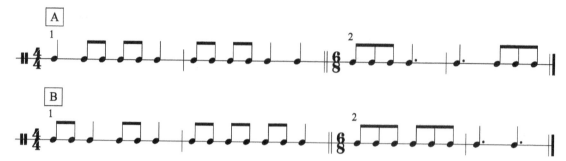

Figure 4.16. Pairs of rhythm patterns in duple and triple meters

Comparing Rhythmic Phrases in Different Meters

To compare rhythmic phrases in different meters, follow a process similar to the one you used with rhythm patterns in different meters. Using the repertoire with which students are familiar, chant two phrases on neutral syllables in the same meter or different meters. For example, perform the first phrase of "Engine, Engine Number Nine" in duple meter and the second phrase of the chant in triple meter. Ask students whether the phrases are the same or different. Then, question them about the meters they are audiating: What meter are you audiating for the first phrase? The second phrase? How do you know the first phrase was in duple meter and the second phrase was in triple meter? Have students use rhythm syllables and movement to demonstrate their answers. For this activity, you could also perform both phrases in duple or triple meter.

Discriminating between patterns in one meter is the goal of the following activity. Students will learn to compare rhythm patterns and functionally use rhythm syllables to demonstrate their comprehension of meter.

Try This!
Rhythm Discrimination

FOCUS

Discriminating between patterns in one meter

PREPARE

"Early to Bed"
Dots large enough to hold in your hand with one color on one side and another color on the other side

ANIMATE

Pass out one colored dot to each student. Tell students that after you chant two rhythm patterns they are to show whether they were the same by matching the color of the dot or different by matching different colored dots with another student. Perform the chant, and at the end, chant two pairs of rhythm patterns in triple meter. If the patterns are the same, students match the same-colored dot with another student. If they are different, students pair opposite colors. Ask individual students questions such as why they chose same or different as their answer, what pitches they were audiating, and what meter they were audiating and why. Have students justify their answers by chanting their responses on rhythm syllables.

ASSESS

Students will be informally assessed with regard to their comprehension of same and different rhythm patterns and the labeling of those patterns.

Discrimination through Repertoire

When students are comfortable discriminating between tonalities and between meters, begin combining them using familiar and unfamiliar repertoire. Perform pairs of phrases of familiar repertoire for students, inviting them to identify whether the repertoire is in the same or different tonality or meter. For example, can students discriminate between "Joshua Fit the Battle of Jericho" when sung in minor and when sung in major? What about the Mozart Sonata Theme in duple and in and triple meters? In the same way, ask your students if they are audiating what they hear as the same or different with other familiar repertoire such as a phrase of "Snake Dance" (minor) paired with phrase of "Mary Ann" (major). Ask students to discern and describe why they are different and use solfège and rhythm skills to justify their responses.

Similarly, perform pairs of familiar chants for students, inviting them to identify whether the meter is the same or different. For example, can students discriminate between "Engine, Engine Number Nine" when performed in duple meter and in triple meter or "Early to Bed" performed in triple and duple meters? Question students about the two meters and have them use rhythm syllables and movement to demonstrate their answers.

Continue to introduce unfamiliar repertoire to your students. Select interesting songs and chants that complement and contrast with the repertoire you are currently teaching. Extending student learning in this way will improve and refine their discrimination skills, leading to audiation-based improvisation.

Additional Techniques for Discrimination

You may wish to use a variety of techniques for students to demonstrate whether the patterns and music they are audiating are the same or different. In addition to Hoops and Dots, two techniques that are explained in the Try This! activities, here are other ways to engage students in Discrimination:

Stand Up or Sit Down

- Ask students to stand when the music they are audiating is the same and to sit down when the music is different.

Thumbs Up or Down

- Invite students to demonstrate same and different by holding a thumb up for same and sideways for different.

Application Cards

- Use index cards that have the word *same* on one side and *different* on the other. After performing patterns for students have them hold up the side of the card that matches what they audiated: same or different.

Move and Freeze

- Ask students to move as a song or chant is performed. At certain points in the music, pause your performance, which is an indication that students are to freeze in place. While students are frozen and silent, perform discrimination patterns and invite them to identify whether the patterns they are audiating are the same or different. Resume the song or chant and repeat the activity.

Same and Different Assessment

- Determine the discrimination activity in which you will involve
  your students. Set either a tonal or a rhythmic context and perform the steps for teaching the activity. Then, provide students
  with a piece of paper with lines numbered from 1 to 5 with
  both *S* (same) and *D* (different) on each line. Present students
  with five discrimination examples, one for each number. Ask
  students to circle *S* or *D* depending on whether they were
  audiating the patterns as the same or different. (See Chapter 7
  for more assessment strategies.)

As you become comfortable teaching discrimination activities, be
creative and compose your own patterns and phrases based on the repertoire you are teaching.

When students can successfully identify same and different musical
content, they are ready to make musical choices. Grounded in listening,
grown in imitation, and now enhanced with the ability to identify same
and different in music, students can create their own music in context
and with understanding.

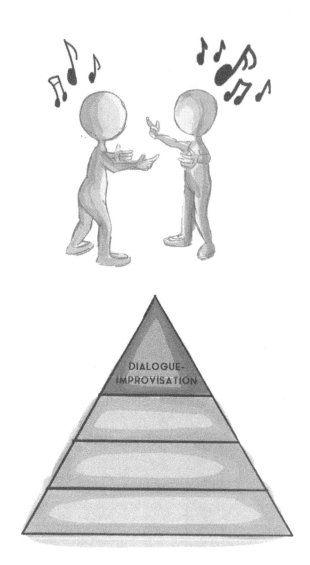

· 5 ·

DIALOGUE-IMPROVISATION

IMPROVISATION IN MUSIC IS analogous to conversation in language.[1] Just as persons speak spontaneously within a context of conversation, so is improvisation a spontaneous interaction between improvisers, musicians, and the repertoire inspiring their musical conversation. Dialogue-Improvisation occurs when students create music in the moment in melodic, harmonic, and rhythmic contexts. Through Dialogue-Improvisation, the top level of the pyramid, students demonstrate comprehension of musical concepts and skills acquired by Listening, Dialogue-Imitation, and Discrimination. Whereas, in the Discrimination process students were asked to identify *same* and *different* melodic patterns, in Dialogue-Improvisation they now engage in *different*, improvising their own music in the moment. When students can improvise their own rhythms, melodic and harmonic patterns, and melodies in context, they are creating their own music with comprehension.[2]

Whole-Part-Whole Approach

In Dialogue-Improvisation, the first *whole* comprises the application of previously learned repertoire to establish tonal and rhythmic contexts for melodic, harmonic, and rhythmic improvisation. Students are engaged in the *part* of improvisation through Dialogue-Imitation (*same*) and Discrimination (*same and different*). The final *whole* is the culmination of all processes in the sequence: Dialogue-Improvisation.[3]

When students begin to improvise, they combine melodic, harmonic, and rhythmic elements of music. Solfège and rhythm syllables function as tools for helping students learn musical content and label what they are audiating. In order to avoid confusion resulting from the use of solfège with rhythm or rhythm syllables with pitches, scaffold instruction so that students gradually move from using solfège and rhythm syllables to using neutral syllables.

Group or Individual Improvisation?
Consider having students sing or chant their improvisations as a class, then ask individuals to improvise their responses. This will allow students an opportunity to audiate and sing or chant *different* before individuals share their musical ideas. Whole-class improvisations may not always sound pleasing to the ear, but they will incite higher-order thinking in music.

Melodic Improvisation

Improvising Melodic Patterns

To begin improvising melodic patterns, establish a major or minor tonal context with repertoire and sing several melodic patterns on solfège in that tonality for students to imitate. Then, sing melodic patterns and invite students to sing a *different* response on solfège. Use the hand signal technique to show students *same* when inviting them to imitate your patterns and *different* when they are to improvise. Allow students a momentary breath between your pattern and theirs. This will help them audiate and construct their responses. At this time, do not be concerned with the melodic content that students sing as much as whether they comprehend the concept of creating a pattern that is unlike yours. Figures 5.1 and 5.2 show a *T* for when you, the teacher will sing and *S* when students should respond.

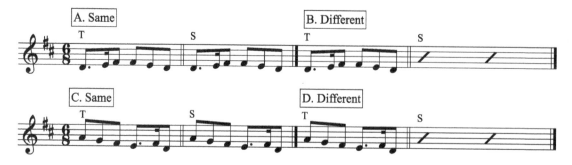

Figure 5.1. Improvising major melodic patterns: Theme from Mozart's Piano Sonata in A (K. 331)

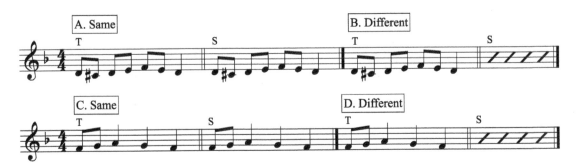

Figure 5.2. Improvising minor melodic patterns: "Joshua Fit the Battle of Jericho"

Figure 5.3. Improvising pairs of major melodic patterns: Theme from Mozart's Piano Sonata in A (K. 331)

Improvising Pairs of Melodic Patterns in One Tonality

Now that your students have created patterns that are different, extend the process to pairs of melodic patterns (see figures 5.3 and 5.4). Establish major or minor tonality and continue singing patterns on solfège. Encourage students to think about how they might make their pair of patterns similar in tonality, meter, and style, yet different from the pair that you perform.

Figure 5.4. Improvising pairs of minor melodic patterns: "Joshua Fit the Battle of Jericho"

Completing Melodic Phrases in One Tonality

After establishing major tonality, teach students the phrase form of the Mozart Sonata Theme (A-A'). On neutral syllables, sing the first phrase of the theme (see figure 5.5) for students, labeling the first half "a" and the second half "b." Sing the second phrase, identifying the first half as "a" and second half as "c." (Note that the first halves are the same and the second halves are different.) Once students learn the phrase form, sing the song again and invite students to complete phrase "c" on solfège. Then, have your students sing the entire song and their improvisations of "c" on neutral syllables. Repeat the same process for "Joshua Fit the Battle of Jericho" (figure 5.6), which has the same phrase form as the Mozart Theme. Remind students to complete the songs with phrases that are similar in tonality, meter, and style to the repertoire. As an extension of this activity, invite students to improvise the first half (a) and then sing the original second half.

The objective of the following activity is to help the class improvise a melody. Students will sing a song in two parts and learn how to improvise an ending to a song.

Figure 5.5. Completing phrases in major tonality: Theme from Mozart's Piano Sonata in A (K. 331)

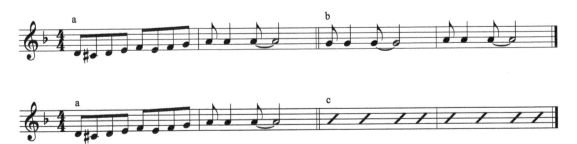

Figure 5.6. Completing phrases in minor tonality: "Joshua Fit the Battle of Jericho"

Try This!
Solo Melodic Improvisation

FOCUS

Individual students improvise a melodic ending to a song in minor tonality and duple meter

PREPARE

"Joshua Fit the Battle of Jericho"
Bean bag
7 to 10 minutes of class time

ANIMATE

Invite students to sit on the floor or at their seats in a circle. After establishing minor tonality and duple meter with a tune-up, have the group sing the melody and bass line of "Joshua Fit the Battle of Jericho" on neutral syllables. Ask the class to sing the bass line while you sing the song, improvising an ending to the song. Inform students that the song is composed of two phrases (A and A'). Sing the first phrase and label it A. Sing the second phrase, labeling it as A'. Invite students to share the reasons why the phrases are different (they have different endings). Divide the class in half and have one group sing the bass line while the other sings the melody. After the group sings the first part of the A' phrase, ask those who are singing the melody to improvise an ending while the bass part continues. Have students switch parts. Pass a bean bag around the circle while the class sings the melody and the bass line. When the group sings the first part of the A' phrase, ask those who are singing the melody to stop singing while the bass part continues. At this point, the student with the bean bag sings an improvised ending. Continue passing the bean bag around the circle so that other students may have a turn improvising an ending. Alternate the groups that sing the bass line and the melody.

ASSESS

Assess individual students with regard to the content of their improvisations. Did the student's improvisation end on the tonic? Did the student sing within the tonality and meter of the song? Did the student improvise with a sense of style?

Harmonic Improvisation

Improvising Harmonic Patterns in One Chord Function

Begin by setting a major or minor tonal context. Perform individual tonic patterns and ask students to either imitate the patterns (*same*) or improvise new ones (*different*) on solfège. Using same and different hand signals will help students know whether they should imitate or improvise a response to your pattern. Figures 5.7 and 5.8 present tonic patterns in major and minor tonalities, respectively. As students become comfortable with improvising within one function, have them improvise on dominant seventh and subdominant functions in one tonality.

Improvising Harmonic Patterns within One Tonality

Establish major or minor tonal context. Next, sing harmonic function patterns (see figures 4.9 and 4.10 from Chapter 4) on solfège in that tonality for students to imitate, and ask them to identify their functions. Then, using the same order of patterns, ask students to sing something different on solfège within a given function. Sing the first pattern (tonic) of the harmonic function patterns, and using chord function signals, gesture for students to breathe and sing a different tonic pattern combination. Sing the second pattern for students and ask them to sing a different subdominant combination, for the third pattern, a different dominant seventh

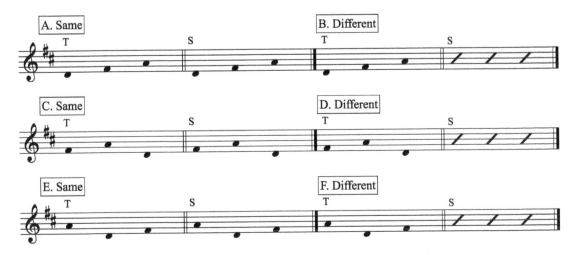

Figure 5.7. Harmonic improvisation: Tonic patterns in major tonality

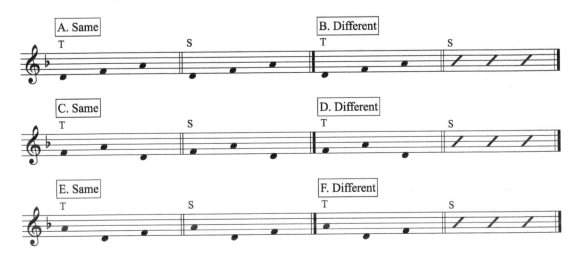

Figure 5.8. Harmonic improvisation: Tonic patterns in minor tonality

combination, and so on until you reach the end of the pattern sequence. This activity builds students' readiness to audiate and track a harmonically interesting improvised idea while sustaining the harmonic progression of a song.

Continue working with students to improvise both tonic, dominant, and subdominant functions (see figures 5.9 and 5.10). Use chord function signals to indicate on which functions students should improvise. As students become flexible in their harmonic improvisations, introduce a variety of progressions, including those from repertoire students are learning.

To indicate *same* (Dialogue-Imitation) and *different* (Dialogue-Improvisation), use the hand signals as previously described. For improvisation on specific chord functions, hold up one finger for tonic, four fingers for subdominant, and five for the dominant-seventh function. Be certain to breathe between patterns so that students have time to audiate and construct their responses.

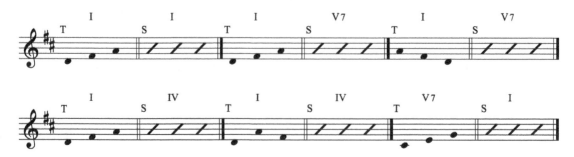

Figure 5.9. Improvising harmonic functions: Major tonality

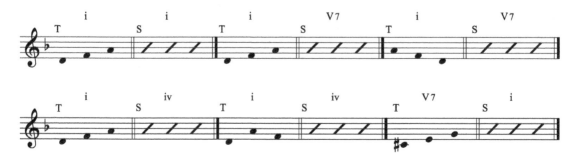

Figure 5.10. Improvising harmonic functions: Minor tonality

Improvising Harmonic Progressions

After teaching students several chord progressions in one tonality (see figures 5.11 and 5.12), invite them to audiate and create patterns that align with those progressions. Teach students to improvise chord progressions with the assistance of chord function signals. Create your own progressions using tonic, dominant, and subdominant functions in major and minor tonalities.

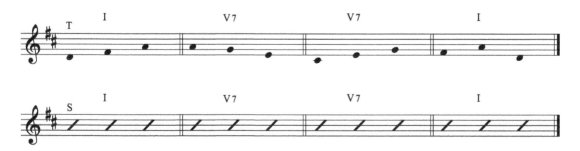

Figure 5.11. Improvising harmonic progressions: Major tonality

Figure 5.12. Improvising harmonic progressions: Minor tonality

Improvising Bass Lines

Review "Joshua Fit the Battle of Jericho" and its corresponding bass line, which is given in figure 5.13, with your students. Ask students to improvise one chord tone per macrobeat, then two chord tones on the microbeat. Using chord function signals, indicate the chord on which students are to improvise. Remind them to audiate the melody while performing the improvised bass line. Teach the Mozart Sonata Theme bass line (figure 5.14) in a similar fashion.

As your students become comfortable improvising harmonic patterns, follow rules of good voice leading. Continue to perform melodies and bass lines with your students, taking note of how characteristic tones accentuate the melody and outline harmonic patterns within the repertoire.

Rhythmic Improvisation

Improvising Rhythm Patterns in One Meter

After chanting a tune-up in triple or duple meter, perform individual patterns on rhythm syllables and ask students to either imitate (*same*) or improvise (*different*) a pattern in that rhythmic context. Use hand signals to help students know whether they should imitate or improvise in response to your pattern. Maintain meter and time when gesturing to students. Figure 5.15 and figure 5.16 present pattern improvisation on macrobeats and microbeats in triple meter and duple meter, respectively.

Improvising Pairs of Rhythm Patterns in One Meter

When students are comfortable improvising individual patterns, combine patterns to form pairs. Repeat the instructional process you followed with individual rhythm patterns. Figures 5.17 and 5.18 present pairs of rhythm patterns to be imitated and improvised.

Figure 5.13. Bass line and improvised example: "Joshua Fit the Battle of Jericho"

Improvising Rhythmic Phrases in One Meter

Inspired by chants or rhythmically interesting repertoire, students should strive to become comfortable improvising chants and rhythms based on the repertoire they are learning. Use the rhythms from familiar repertoire (figures 5.19 and 5.20) as antecedent phrases and invite students to improvise their own consequent phrases. Figure 5.19 is based on the rhythm of "Engine, Engine, Number Nine," and figure 5.20 is based on the rhythm of "Early to Bed."

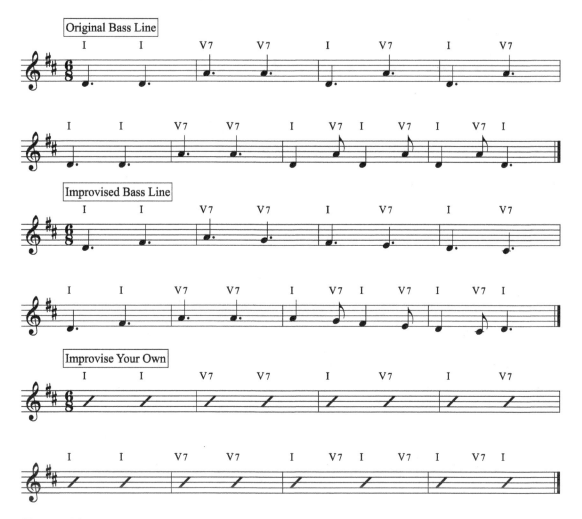

Figure 5.14. Bass line and improvised example: Theme from Mozart's Piano Sonata in A (K. 331)

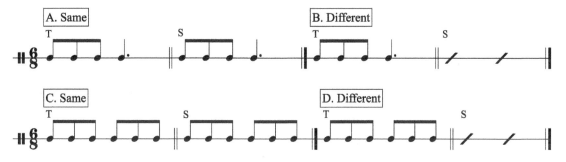

Figure 5.15. Improvising rhythm patterns: Triple meter

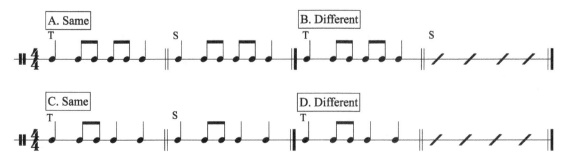

Figure 5.16. Improvising rhythm patterns: Duple meter

Figure 5.17. Improvising pairs of rhythm patterns: Triple meter

Figure 5.18. Improvising pairs of rhythm patterns: Duple meter

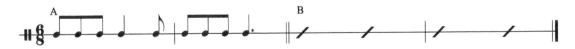

Figure 5.19. Completing phrases in triple meter: "Early to Bed"

Figure 5.20. Completing phrases in duple meter: "Engine, Engine, Number nine"

The following lesson presents an activity in which students improvise an ostinato to accompany a chant. Not only do students chant in two parts, but they also become fluent with improvising rhythm patterns.

Try This!

From Ostinato to Accompaniment

FOCUS

Improvise ostinati to create an accompaniment for a chant

PREPARE

"Engine, Engine Number Nine"
7 to 10 minutes of class time

ANIMATE

Review "Engine, Engine Number Nine" with students. Invite half of the class to perform the chant and the other half to perform a macrobeat ostinato. Switch parts. Engage students in call and response with duple meter patterns using rhythm syllables. Chant a four-macrobeat pattern for the class and invite students to chant the *same* pattern. Perform a four-macrobeat pattern for the class but this time ask students to chant a four-macrobeat pattern that is *different*. Ask individual students to perform their patterns for the class, and have the class imitate them. Use students' improvised patterns to develop ostinati for the chant. Have half of the class perform the chant while the other half performs the ostinato. Continue this activity, encouraging students to improvise patterns to accompany the chant.

ASSESS

Assess individual students with regard to their ability to improvise a four-macrobeat rhythm pattern in the meter and tempo of the original chant.

Improvisation Activities

As students begin to improvise, remind them to use neutral syllables and to maintain the style, meter, tempo, and tonality of the music on which they are basing their improvisation. Vary instruction to provide opportunities for the whole group, small groups, and individual students to share their improvisations with you. The following activities scaffold students' ability to combine melodic, harmonic, and rhythmic content, ultimately supporting their efforts to improvise spontaneously.

Call and Response

- Establish musical dialogue by reviewing Dialogue-Imitation activities.
- Perform a pattern and invite students to improvise a pattern.
- Invite individual students to perform a pattern that the class imitates.
- Invite individual students to perform a pattern on which the class improvises.
- Pair up students and invite them to practice both calling and responding to each other.

Antecedent-Consequent Improvisation

- As a group, sing a well-known song and its bass line.
- Divide the class in half. Ask one group to sing the bass line and the other group the melody of the song. Switch parts.
- Teach students the phrase form of the music and determine where the antecedent and consequent phrases are.
- Sing the first full phrase and ask students to audiate an improvisation that is in the same tonality, meter, and style for the second phrase.
- Sing the first full phrase again and ask students to sing an improvisation that is in the same tonality, meter, and style for the second phrase.
- Ask students to audiate an improvisation for the first full phrase and to sing the second phrase.
- Improvise the first phrase and sing the second phrase as a group.
- Improvise both phrases as a group.
- Invite individual students to improvise both phrases while the class sings the bass line.

Melody over Bass Line

- Invite your students to sing a song they know well.
- Sing the bass line and ask students to audiate a different melody.
- Sing the bass line and ask students to improvise a melody on neutral syllables.
- Invite individual students to improvise a melody.
- Encourage students to improvise their melodies in a variety of tonalities, meters, tempos, and styles.

Melody and Bass Line

- Invite your students to sing a song they know well.
  Divide the class in half. Ask one group to sing the bass line of the song and the other group to sing the melody, on neutral syllables. Switch parts.
- Ask one group to improvise on the bass line while the other sings the melody. Switch parts.
- Ask one group to improvise on the bass line and the other to improvise a melody. Switch parts.
- Invite pairs of students to improvise on bass lines and melodies.
- Encourage students to improvise in a variety of tonalities, meters, tempos, and styles.

Culminating Activity

Invite students to improvise melodies and accompaniments in the tonality, meter, style, and form of familiar repertoire. Figures 5.21 and 5.22 present the melody, an example of an improvised melody, slash notation, and chord symbols for the Mozart Sonata Theme and "Joshua Fit the Battle of Jericho," respectively. Invite small groups of students to create arrangements of the original song, with variations of the melody and bass line. Ask students to include an introduction and coda. Have them perform their arrangements for the class.

Figure 5.21. Improvisation in the style of the theme from Mozart's Piano Sonata in A (K. 331)

Be flexible and spontaneous with students while they are improvising. Provide feedback in the moment about what was most interesting about their improvisations and return to either melodic, harmonic, or rhythmic activities based on your assessment of students' musical needs.

Improvisation is higher-order thinking in music through which students use the foundation you have provided and their inference skills to improvise. Having readiness to

Figure 5.22. Improvisation in the style of "Joshua Fit the Battle of Jericho"

improvise gained from the processes of Listening, Dialogue-Imitation, and Discrimination, students are prepared to create unique musical content within a music context, spontaneously. This is the final *whole* of the improvisation sequence and the final level of the pyramid: Dialogue-Improvisation!

· 6 ·

APPLICATION TO INSTRUMENTS

SINGING, CHANTING, AND MOVING to music form the foundation for all instrumental music instruction. Through these activities, students connect their audiation with the music they play on their instruments. This is the same whether students are learning to play new music or are improvising.[1] With this in mind, the purpose of this chapter is to provide pedagogical techniques for transferring and applying the improvisation process presented in Chapters 2 through 5 to instruments.

General Principles for Applying Audiation to Instruments

Connecting Singing to Instruments

Connecting students' audiation instrument to their physical instrument is critical to helping them improvise. To audiate the music they improvise, students need to sing and chant what they play and play what they sing and chant. When your students can sing repertoire that will be transferred to instruments, ask them to sing that repertoire while playing their *imaginary* instruments. This allows you to visually check students' executive skills (for example, hand placement, posture, and holding position) before they play real instruments. Next, have students hold their actual instruments and sing while practicing executive skills such as fingerings. For example, invite wind players to blow air through their instruments while fingering and articulating the music. Finally, ask students to perform the music on their instruments.

Because beginning students will be limited in the number of pitches they can play, instruct them to sing and play the tonic of the repertoire you are teaching or are about to teach. Then, add new pitches in context. For example, once students can perform *do, re,* and *mi* for simple major tonality songs, add *ti* so they can play simple tonic-dominant bass lines. Similarly, once students can perform *la, ti,* and *do* for songs in minor tonality, add *si* for minor tonic-dominant bass lines.

Range is one of the most important considerations when transferring music from voice to instruments. Sing patterns in a comfortable key (C and D usually work well). Next, establish tonality in the instrument key, which may be different. Then, invite students to perform the same patterns in the new key on their instruments. Consider using your own instrument to model performing in multiple keys.

As students learn new pitches, teach them to sing and perform melodic and harmonic patterns on their instruments in call-and-response form (see Chapter 2 for melodic and harmonic pattern sequences). Extract melodic patterns from familiar repertoire and consider introducing melodic patterns from the repertoire you plan on teaching. Use harmonic patterns to reinforce instrument fingerings and tonalities in which students are performing. Consider integrating pattern instruction into an instrumental warm-up, focusing on the tonality of repertoire students are learning. If you have a long rehearsal block, incorporate pattern instruction between pieces. This serves as a good change of pace and an opportunity to help students audiate the tonality or key of the next piece of repertoire.

Connecting Rhythm to Instruments

Movement constitutes readiness for chanting and performing rhythms. Therefore, engage your students in movement activities before they get out their instruments. Establish two types of movement for your students: macrobeats and microbeats. Have students move their heels to the macrobeats and feel the microbeats by patting their thighs or their shoulders. You may also invite students to rock back and forth in their chairs to the macrobeat. Now that students are moving, involve them in rhythm pattern instruction in the meter of the music they will play (see Chapter 2 for rhythm pattern sequences). Rhythm patterns are excellent for warm-ups. Invite students to imitate patterns with a variety of articulations on a comfortable pitch, perhaps the tonic of the key in which they are about to play. When students are comfortable moving in time, they are ready to perform rhythms on instruments.

After moving to the macrobeat and microbeat of the music they will play, ask students to hold their instruments and chant rhythms on the air stream. Be sure the articulation that you and your students use (such as connected versus separated articulation) matches the style of the repertoire they are learning. Next, invite your students to perform rhythm patterns on a single pitch such as the tonic of the music. It is important to stay on the same pitch for rhythm pattern instruction so that students focus on rhythmic content of the patterns.

Applying Instrumental Principles to the Improvisation Sequence

Recommendations for application of the improvisation sequence to instrumental music instruction are organized by the Listening, Dialogue-Imitation, Discrimination, and Dialogue-Improvisation processes presented earlier. The first process frames the initial step toward instrumental improvisation.

Listening

Involve your students in listening activities. Provide listening opportunities by playing recordings as students enter the classroom. During rehearsals or classes, play recorded examples of the repertoire that students are learning to help them internalize concepts such as tone, articulation, and style. Share professional-caliber recordings that feature the instruments students are studying and provide links to recordings that they may listen to independently.

Dialogue-Imitation

Invite students to imitate your musical model. A natural and important extension of listening activities is to invite students to echo you on their instruments. Apply Dialogue-Imitation activities suggested in Chapter 3 to instrumental instruction. Sing and chant for students and ask students to imitate you. Next, perform on an instrument for students and have them imitate your model, paying attention to intonation, expression, and style. Engage students in Dialogue-Imitation on instruments during warm-ups, between pieces, or as a teaching activity while rehearsing a piece. Be sure to balance the singing or chanting of patterns with playing them on instruments, being mindful of the range, key, and complexity of the music.

Discrimination

Teach same and different. In Discrimination, students learn to differentiate between same and different musical content, ultimately understanding that *different* leads to improvisation. Perform same and different melodic, harmonic, and rhythm patterns for students (see Chapter 4 for Discrimination techniques). Invite students to discern whether the patterns were the same or different.

Dialogue-Improvisation

Facilitate students' improvisations. When improvising, instrumentalists connect all of the aforementioned processes to spontaneously create new content within a musical context. With the other Dialogue-Improvisation activities presented in Chapter 5, continue having students sing or chant their musical ideas before performing them on instruments. This technique helps clarify whether students are transferring the musical content they are audiating to their instruments. Should a student have trouble performing his or her musical ideas, work with that student to identify gaps in executive skills (for example, a new fingering) that may be preventing the student from performing the improvisation.

Improvising on musical instruments is rewarding for students of all ages. By following the improvisation sequence presented in Chapters 2 through 5, your students will be prepared to transfer their improvisatory skills to a musical instrument of any kind.

• 7 •

ASSESSMENT

ASSESSMENT IS CRITICAL TO music teaching and learning. It helps determine if your students are learning what you think you taught them.[1] Through assessment, you will find out how well your students have learned musical concepts and skills and how to adjust your instruction to meet their musical needs. Improvisation provides an ideal means to learn what your students have achieved musically and assess their musical comprehension.[2]

Assessment should be aligned with learning goals and objectives within a curricular framework. Figure 7.1 presents a scope and sequence for the processes of Listening, Dialogue-Imitation, Discrimination, and Dialogue-Improvisation. The scope and sequence assumes twenty-five class meetings and divides class time evenly among the repertoire presented throughout the book: the Mozart Sonata Theme, "Joshua Fit the Battle of Jericho," "Engine, Engine Number Nine," and "Early to Bed."

As a general rule, when 80 percent of the class has achieved success in meeting your objectives, move forward with your instruction.

After acculturating your students to new repertoire in week one, introduce Dialogue-Imitation with neutral syllables to your students in weeks two and three. Then, in week four or five, assess your students' ability to imitate melodic, harmonic, and rhythm patterns on neutral syllables. This assessment will help you pace your instruction before progressing to Dialogue-Imitation with solfège or rhythm syllables. It is possible that students may be ready to move to the next process more

Week	"Mozart Sonata Theme"	"Joshua Fit the Battle of Jericho"	"Old Joe Clark"	"Engine, Engine, Number 9"	"Early to Bed"	"Dessert"
Tonality/ Meter	Major/Triple	Minor/Duple	Mixolydian/ Duple	Duple	Triple	Asymmetrical
1	Listen	Listen	Listen	Listen	Listen	Listen
2	Dialogue-Imitation (Neutral Syllables)	Listen	Listen	Dialogue-Imitation (Neutral Syllables)	Listen	Listen
3		Dialogue-Imitation (Neutral Syllables)	Teach Song		Dialogue-Imitation (Neutral Syllables)	Teach Chant
	(Introduce new repertoire to the Listening process)					
4	Dialogue-Imitation (Neutral Syllables)			Dialogue-Imitation (Neutral Syllables)		
5		Dialogue-Imitation (Neutral Syllables)			Dialogue-Imitation (Neutral Syllables)	
6	Dialogue-Imitation (Solfege)			Dialogue-Imitation (Rhythm Syllables)		
7		Dialogue-Imitation (Solfege)			Dialogue-Imitation (Rhythm Syllables)	
8	Dialogue-Imitation (Solfege)			Dialogue-Imitation (Rhythm Syllables)		
9		Dialogue-Imitation (Solfege)			Dialogue-Imitation (Rhythm Syllables)	
	(Introduce new repertoire to the Listening process)					
10	Dialogue-Imitation (Solfege)			Dialogue-Imitation (Rhythm Syllables)		
11		Dialogue-Imitation (Solfege)			Dialogue-Imitation (Rhythm Syllables)	
12	Discrimination			Discrimination		
	(Introduce new repertoire to the Listening process)					
13		Discrimination			Discrimination	
14	Discrimination			Discrimination		
15		Discrimination			Discrimination	

Figure 7.1. Projected scope and sequence over twenty-five weeks of instruction

Week	"Mozart Sonata Theme"	"Joshua Fit the Battle of Jericho"	"Old Joe Clark"	"Engine, Engine, Number 9"	"Early to Bed"	"Dessert"
16	Discrimination			Discrimination		
17		Discrimination			Discrimination	
18	Dialogue-Improvisation (Solfege)			Dialogue-Improvisation (Rhythm Syllables)		
(Introduce new repertoire to the Listening process)						
19		Dialogue-Improvisation (Solfege)			Dialogue-Improvisation (Rhythm Syllables)	
20	Dialogue-Improvisation (Solfege)			Dialogue-Improvisation (Rhythm Syllables)		
21		Dialogue-Improvisation (Solfege)			Dialogue-Improvisation (Rhythm Syllables)	
22	Dialogue-Improvisation (Neutral Syllables)			Dialogue-Improvisation (Neutral Syllables)		
23		Dialogue-Improvisation (Neutral Syllables)			Dialogue-Improvisation (Neutral Syllables)	
24	Dialogue-Improvisation (Neutral Syllables)			Dialogue-Improvisation (Neutral Syllables)		
(Introduce new repertoire to the Listening process)						
25		Dialogue-Improvisation (Neutral Syllables)			Dialogue-Improvisation (Neutral Syllables)	

Figure 7.1. Continued

quickly than you planned; sometimes they will need more time to demonstrate comprehension of the content you are teaching.

Formative and Summative Assessment

Music teachers engage in assessment all of the time. As your students demonstrate musical achievement such as accuracy of imitating melodic patterns, you naturally make a mental note to the effect that "they did it" or "they did not do it." Formative assessment serves as a catalyst for providing students with ongoing feedback. It gives you instant feedback based on the performance of your students, and helps you gauge the effectiveness of your instruction.

While formative assessment takes place regularly throughout instruction, summative assessment occurs at the end of a unit, marking period, semester, or academic year. Summative assessment is cumulative in nature, providing a means to track student achievement related to overarching outcomes as documented in your scope and sequence. For example, you might engage in summative assessment when students have learned duple and triple meter macrobeat and microbeat patterns with rhythm syllables. By means of this assessment you can determine whether your students are ready to move to the next process, Discrimination. Documenting your students' learning and growth through formative and summative assessment is a powerful way to support the music teaching and learning process.

Overview of Assessment Techniques

It is important to begin with a clear picture of the learning goals and objectives of your curriculum: What concepts and skills should your students know and be able to perform? For guidance, refer to your scope and sequence which provides you with direction for defining student learning outcomes. With these outcomes as a frame, create an assessment tool with which to document student achievement.

Keep evaluations simple at first and think about the assessment of learning as a progression of simple to complex decisions you make when evaluating student performance. These are questions you may want to ask yourself: Are students accurately chanting duple meter rhythm patterns? Are they accurately performing the bass line to the Mozart Sonata Theme? Are students correctly discriminating between major and minor tonalities? Consider the following strategies for creating assessments: checklists, additive rating scales, continuous rating scales, and rubrics. Strive to use positive, active language in your assessments, avoiding words such as *wrong* or *missed*. Instead, use adjectives such as *few, some, most,* and *all.* These language choices remind students that measurement and evaluation should be a positive, not negative, experience.

Checklists

Using a checklist is an effective step toward providing a quick snap-shot of how many students are achieving a given objective. To create a checklist, break down objectives to basic yes-or-no questions: Did your students do what they were asked to do or not? Did students accurately perform a given song or chant? Did they improvise in the tonality, meter, and style of "Joshua Fit the Battle of Jericho"?

Identify content you wish to assess and create a checklist that includes students' names and the content being assessed. This type of assessment works well for Discrimination activities, in which the student's response is either correct or incorrect. For example, you may have a learning objective that addresses whether students can tell if patterns in triple meter are the same or different (see figure 7.2). As students respond to the given objective, write a checkmark by their names on the checklist. Count the check marks on your list. If 80 percent of students are achieving the objective, the class is ready to move on to the next activity or process.

Check the box when student successfully discriminates between same and different triple meter rhythm patterns.

Student	✓
Anna	☐
Boyd	☐
Henry	☐
Mike	☐
Zoe	☐

Figure 7.2. Checklist for discriminating between same and different triple meter rhythmic patterns

Additive Rating Scales

Use additive rating scales to assess several criteria related to one objective. One objective might address having your students improvise a melody in minor tonality and triple meter. An additive rating scale could include the following criteria: singing in tune, singing with a sense of style, maintaining a sense of tonality, maintaining a sense of meter, and maintaining a sense of time (see figure 7.3). Students earn points for each criterion they successfully achieve.

Student earns one point for successfully achieving each of the following criteria:

Criteria	Student:	Anna	Boyd	Henry	Mike	Zoe
Singing in Tune		—	—	—	—	—
Singing with a Sense of Style		—	—	—	—	—
Maintaining a Sense of Tonality		—	—	—	—	—
Maintaining a Sense of Meter		—	—	—	—	—
Maintaining a Sense of Time		—	—	—	—	—

Figure 7.3. Additive rating scale for improvising a melody in minor tonality and triple meter

Continuous Rating Scales

As you become comfortable with evaluating students using checklists and additive rating scales, expand your criteria to 4- or 5-point rating scales. Continuous rating scales represent a hierarchy of student achievement and should focus on specific musical content. (For example, a rhythm rating scale would not include tonal criteria.) Continuous rating scales may be used for objectives that address students' achievement with Dialogue-Imitation or Dialogue-Improvisation activities. Figure 7.4 presents a continuous rating scale for an objective related to improvising with rhythm syllables in a steady tempo.

Student must achieve the first criteria before moving on to the second criteria.

Student's improvisation was performed

1   without a sense of meter.

2   with a sense of meter but an unsteady tempo.

3   with a sense of meter and nearly steady tempo.

4   with a sense of meter and steady tempo.

Figure 7.4. Chanting rhythm syllables with a sense of meter and steady tempo

Rubrics

Rubrics combine several rating scales, allowing for measurement of multiple sets of skills that students should demonstrate. They describe a variety of achievement levels. Dimensions for a rubric might document the degree to which students are able to improvise (a) rhythm in triple meter, (b) a melody over a bass line, and (c) harmonic accompaniment to a well-known song. Because music is a multifaceted art form, provide students with feedback on a variety of musical content.

Student Self-Assessment

Student achievement rises when students assess their own work. Invite students to self-assess using the same rating scale or rubric you plan to use to assess their musical achievement. One assignment might be for students to submit recordings of their improvisations along with a self-assessment. Take advantage of your school's learning software platform and publish assignments, including information about how you will assess students' performance. Strive for several summative assessments per year. Imagine the possibilities when your students can track their own growth and you possess powerful student learning data to share with parents, administrators, and other stakeholders!

Once you review and evaluate students' work, be sure to interact with them about the level of agreement between your assessment and theirs. Highlight points where your assessments agree and disagree. Then, hold a brief conference with the student. Strive for an open, evaluative conversation with each student at least once per unit, marking period, or semester.

Formative and summative assessment techniques provide you with an opportunity to measure student progress throughout your curriculum. By prioritizing improvisation in music teaching and learning, you will help your students develop their abilities to audiate and spontaneously create music with understanding.

Appendix

ADDITIONAL SONGS AND CHANTS

In this appendix you will find public domain repertoire gleaned from a variety of sources. Use it to enhance your instruction, remembering that one of the most important things you can do to increase your students' music vocabulary is to teach them as many songs and chants as possible.

Song	Tonality	Meter
All the Pretty Little Horses	Aeolian	Duple
Canoe Song	Aeolian	Duple
Hey Ho! Nobody Home	Aeolian	Duple
Paddy Works on the Railway	Aeolian	Triple
Round and Round	Dorian	Duple
Haul Away, Joe	Dorian	Triple
Abide with Me	Major	Duple
Ach Du Leiber Augustine	Major	Duple
Alabama Gal	Major	Duple
All Night, All Day	Major	Duple
Aloha Oe	Major	Duple
Alouette	Major	Duple
America	Major	Duple
Annie Laurie	Major	Duple
Auld Lang Syne	Major	Duple
Biddy, Biddy	Major	Duple
Bill Bailey	Major	Duple

Song	Tonality	Meter
Bill Grogan's Goat	Major	Duple
Billy Boy	Major	Duple
Blue Bells of Scotland	Major	Duple
Boil Them Cabbages	Major	Duple
Buffalo Gals	Major	Duple
Caisson Song	Major	Duple
Camptown Races	Major	Duple
Can Can from "Orpheus"	Major	Duple
Canon in D	Major	Duple
Carry Me Back to Old Virginny	Major	Duple
Columbia, the Gem of the Ocean	Major	Duple
Dance of the Sugarplum Fairies	Major	Duple
Dayenu	Major	Duple
Deck the Halls	Major	Duple
Diddle, Diddle, Dumpling	Major	Duple
Dixie	Major	Duple
Do, Lord, Remember Me	Major	Duple
Dona Nobis Pacem	Major	Duple
Down by the Riverside	Major	Duple
Eine Kleine Nachtmusik	Major	Duple
Ezekiel Saw the Wheel	Major	Duple
Frere Jacques	Major	Duple
Frosty the Snowman	Major	Duple
Galway Piper	Major	Duple
Go, Tell Aunt Rhody	Major	Duple
Go, Tell It on the Mountain	Major	Duple
Good King Wenceslas	Major	Duple
Grizzly Bear	Major	Duple
He's Got the Whole World in His Hands	Major	Duple
Head and Shoulders, Knees and Toes	Major	Duple
Hey, Betty Martin	Major	Duple
High School Cadets	Major	Duple
I've Been Working on the Railroad	Major	Duple
Jamaican Farewell	Major	Duple
Jingle Bells	Major	Duple

Song	Tonality	Meter
Kookaburra	Major	Duple
Kum Ba Ya	Major	Duple
La Cucaracha	Major	Duple
La Raspa	Major	Duple
Liza Jane	Major	Duple
Loch Lomond	Major	Duple
London Bridge	Major	Duple
Long, Long Ago	Major	Duple
Love Somebody	Major	Duple
Mary Ann	Major	Duple
Mary Had a Little Lamb	Major	Duple
Mexican Hat Dance	Major	Duple
Michael Finnegan	Major	Duple
Michael, Row the Boat Ashore	Major	Duple
Nobody Knows the Trouble I've Seen	Major	Duple
O Danny Boy	Major	Duple
O Susanna!	Major	Duple
Ode to Joy	Major	Duple
Old Joe Tucker	Major	Duple
Old King Cole	Major	Duple
Old MacDonald	Major	Duple
Polly Put the Kettle On	Major	Duple
Polly Wolly Doodle	Major	Duple
Rock-a My Soul	Major	Duple
Sansa Kroma	Major	Duple
Sarasponda	Major	Duple
She'll Be Comin' Round the Mountain	Major	Duple
Shortnin' Bread	Major	Duple
Simple Gifts	Major	Duple
Skip To My Lou	Major	Duple
Sleep, Baby, Sleep	Major	Duple
Sourwood Mountain	Major	Duple
Swanee River	Major	Duple
Tallis's Canon	Major	Duple
The Battle Hymn of the Republic	Major	Duple
The Entertainer	Major	Duple

Song	Tonality	Meter
The Mockingbird	Major	Duple
The Riddle Song	Major	Duple
The Yellow Rose of Texas	Major	Duple
Theme from Brahms's First Symphony	Major	Duple
Theme from "Prince Igor"	Major	Duple
This Little Light of Mine	Major	Duple
This Old Man	Major	Duple
This Train	Major	Duple
Tideo	Major	Duple
Tinga Layo	Major	Duple
Tom Dooley	Major	Duple
Train	Major	Duple
Turkey in the Straw	Major	Duple
Twinkle, Twinkle	Major	Duple
Up on the Housetop	Major	Duple
Vesper Hymn	Major	Duple
We Shall Overcome	Major	Duple
When the Saints Go Marching In	Major	Duple
White Cockle Bells	Major	Duple
William Tell Overture	Major	Duple
Winter Wonderland	Major	Duple
Yankee Doodle Boy	Major	Duple
You Are My Sunshine	Major	Duple
You're a Grand Old Flag	Major	Duple
Bach Minuet in G	Major	Triple
Barbara Allen	Major	Triple
Beautiful Dreamer	Major	Triple
Bicycle Built for Two	Major	Triple
Blue Danube	Major	Triple
Cockles and Mussels	Major	Triple
Cuckoo	Major	Triple
Down in the Valley	Major	Triple
Drink to Me Only with Thine Eyes	Major	Triple
For He's A Jolly Good Fellow	Major	Triple
Hickory Dickory Dock	Major	Triple
Home on the Range	Major	Triple

Song	Tonality	Meter
I'se the B'y	Major	Triple
If You're Happy	Major	Triple
Jesu, Joy of Man's Desiring	Major	Triple
Lavender's Blue	Major	Triple
Liebestraum	Major	Triple
Little Boy Blue	Major	Triple
Little Tom Tinker	Major	Triple
Looby Loo	Major	Triple
Mozart Sonata Theme	Major	Triple
My Bonnie Lies over the Ocean	Major	Triple
My Hat	Major	Triple
Oats, Peas, Beans	Major	Triple
Oh, How Lovely Is the Evening	Major	Triple
On Top of Old Smokey	Major	Triple
Over the River	Major	Triple
Pop Goes the Weasel	Major	Triple
Sally Go 'Round the Sun	Major	Triple
Siyahamba	Major	Triple
The Ash Grove	Major	Triple
The Band Played On	Major	Triple
The Farmer in the Dell	Major	Triple
The Man on the Flying Trapeze	Major	Triple
The Mulberry Bush	Major	Triple
The Star-Spangled Banner	Major	Triple
The Streets of Laredo	Major	Triple
There's a Hole in the Bucket	Major	Triple
There's a Song in the Air	Major	Triple
Three Blind Mice	Major	Triple
Vive L'Amour	Major	Triple
When Irish Eyes Are Smiling	Major	Triple
Where, Oh Where Has My Little Dog Gone?	Major	Triple
Rig a Jig Jig	Major	Duple & Triple
Monkey Song	Major	Mixed
The Banks of Newfoundland	Major	Mixed
Quick Step	Major	Asymmetrical

Song	Tonality	Meter
Yerakina	Major	Asymmetrical
Don Gato	Minor	Duple
Follow the Drinking Gourd	Minor	Duple
Fum, Fum, Fum	Minor	Duple
Go Down, Moses	Minor	Duple
Hatikvah	Minor	Duple
Hava Nagila	Minor	Duple
Joshua Fit the Battle of Jericho	Minor	Duple
Sakura	Minor	Duple
Shalom Chaverim	Minor	Duple
Snake Dance	Minor	Duple
Song from Ancient Karyes	Minor	Duple
The Swan	Minor	Duple
This Old Hammer	Minor	Duple
Volga Boatman	Minor	Duple
Zum Gali Gali	Minor	Duple
Five Cents I Have	Minor	Triple
Tarantella	Minor	Triple
Three Young Men From Volos	Minor	Asymmetrical
Erie Canal	Minor-Major	Duple
I'm Gonna Put on My Walkin' Shoes	Mixolydian	Duple
Old Joe Clark	Mixolydian	Duple
Chants	**Meter**	
Diddle Diddle Dumpling	Duple	
Engine, Engine Number Nine	Duple	
Noble Duke of York	Duple	
Early to Bed	Triple	
Hickory, Dickory Dock	Triple	
Noble Duke of York	Triple	
Dessert	Asymmetrical	
I Hear It Coming (The Train)	Asymmetrical	

NOTES

Chapter 1
1. See Gordon (2011).
2. See Gordon (2012).
3. For more information on Laban, see http://artsalive.ca/en/dan/meet/bios/artistDetail.asp?artistID=175

Chapter 2
1. See Gordon (2012).
2. See Taggart, Bolton, Reynolds, Valerio, & Gordon (2000).
3. See Grunow, Gordon, & Azzara (2001).
4. See Weikart (2006).

Chapter 3
1. See Gordon (2012).
2. https://giml.org/mlt/lsa-rhythmcontent/

Chapter 4
1. See Gordon (2005); Gordon (2012); Grunow, Gordon, & Azzara (2001); Taggart, Bolton, Reynolds, Valerio, & Gordon (2000).

Chapter 5
1. See Azzara (2002).
2. See Gordon (2012); Grunow, Gordon, & Azzara (2001); Taggart, Bolton, Reynolds, Valerio, & Gordon (2000).
3. See Azzara & Grunow (2006, 2010a, 2010b).

Chapter 6

1. See Grunow, Gordon, & Azzara (2001).

Chapter 7

1. See Walters (2010).
2. See Azzara & Grunow (2006, 2010a, 2010b); Gordon (2012); Grunow, Gordon, & Azzara (2001); Taggart (2018).

BIBLIOGRAPHY

ArtsAlive. (2017). *Meet the artists: Rudolph von Laban.* Retrieved from http://artsalive.ca/en/dan/meet/bios/artistDetail.asp?artistID=175

Azzara, C. D. (2002). Improvisation. In R. Colwell & C. Richardson (Eds.), *The new handbook of research on music teaching and learning* (pp. 171–187). New York, NY: Oxford University Press.

Azzara, C. D., & Grunow, R. F. (2006, 2010a, 2010b). *Developing musicianship through improvisation* [Books 1, 2, and 3]. Chicago, IL: GIA.

Burton, S. L., & Reynolds, A. M. (Eds.). (2018). *Engaging musical practices: A sourcebook for elementary general music.* Lanham, MD: Rowman & Littlefield Education. Published in partnership with the National Association for Music Education.

Burton, S. L., & Snell, A. H., II (Eds.). (2015). *Engaging musical practices: A sourcebook for instrumental music.* Lanham, MD: Rowman & Littlefield Education. Published in partnership with the National Association for Music Education.

Burton, S. L., & Townsend, R. D. (2015). Shaping readiness for instrumental music. In S. L. Burton & A. H. Snell II (Eds.), *Engaging musical practices: A sourcebook for instrumental music* (pp. 3–20). Lanham, MD: Rowman & Littlefield Education. Published in partnership with the National Association for Music Education.

Gordon, E. E. (2003). *Improvisation in the music classroom.* Chicago, IL: GIA.

Gordon, E. E. (2005). *Reference handbook for using learning sequence activities.* Chicago, IL: GIA.

Gordon, E. E. (2011). Early childhood music abuse: Misdeeds and neglect. *Visions of Research in Music Education, 17*. Retrieved from http://www--usr.rider.edu/vrme~/

Gordon, E. E. (2012). *Learning sequences in music: A contemporary music learning theory.* Chicago, IL: GIA.

Gordon Institute for Music Learning. (n. d.). *Professional development level courses.* Certification in early childhood music, elementary, elementary general music levels 1 and 2, instrumental music. Retrieved from https://giml.org/pdlc/about/

Grunow, R. F., Gordon, E. E., & Azzara, C. D. (2001). *Jump right in: The instrumental series.* Chicago, IL: GIA.

Higgins, L., & Campbell, P. S. (2010). *Free to be musical: Group improvisation in music.* Lanham, MD: Rowman & Littlefield Education.

Reynolds, A. M., & Burton, S. L. (2016). Serve and return: Communication foundations for early childhood music policy stakeholders. *Arts Education Policy Review, 118*(3), 140–153. doi: 10.1080/10632913.2016.1244779.

Reynolds, A. M., Long, S., & Valerio, W. H. (2007). Language acquisition and music acquisition: Possible parallels. In L. R. Bartel (Series Ed.), K. Smithrim, & R. Upitis (Vol. Eds.), *Listen to their voices. Research to practice: A biennial series* (vol. 3), (pp. 211–227). Waterloo, ON, Canada: Canadian Music Educators Association.

Reynolds, A. M., & Valerio, W. H. (2015). Early childhood music curriculum. In C. Conway (Ed.), *Musicianship-focused curriculum and assessment* (pp. 329–366). Chicago, IL: GIA.

Runfola, M., & Taggart, C. C. (Eds.). (2005). *Development and practical application of music learning theory.* Chicago, IL: GIA.

Shouldice, H. (2018). Audiation-based improvisation and composition in elementary general music. In S. L. Burton & A. M. Reynolds (Eds.), *Engaging musical practices: A sourcebook for elementary general music* (pp. 113–134). Lanham, MD: Rowman & Littlefield Education. Published in partnership with the National Association for Music Education.

Snell, A. H., II (2015). Teaching everybody everything. In S. L. Burton & A. H. Snell, II (Eds.), *Engaging musical practices: A sourcebook for instrumental music* (pp. 163–180). Lanham, MD: Rowman & Littlefield Education.

Stringham, D. A. (2015). Engaging students in instrumental music assessment. In S. L. Burton and A. H. Snell, II (Eds.), *Engaging musical practices: A sourcebook for instrumental music* (pp. 199–216). Lanham, MD: Rowman & Littlefield.

Taggart, C. C. (2018). Getting to know our students: Assessment in the elementary general music classroom. In S. L. Burton & A. M. Reynolds (Eds.), *Engaging musical practices: A sourcebook for elementary general music* (pp. 237–252). Lanham, MD: Rowman & Littlefield Education. Published in partnership with the National Association for Music Education.

Taggart, C. C., Bolton, B. M., Reynolds, A. M., Valerio, W. H., & Gordon, E. E. (2000). *Jump right in: The general music curriculum.* Chicago, IL: GIA.

Valerio, W. H., Reynolds, A. M., Bolton, B. M., Taggart, C. C., & Gordon, E. E. (1998). *Music play.* Chicago, IL: GIA.

Walters, D. (2010). *A concise guide to assessing skill and knowledge with music achievement as a model.* Chicago, IL: GIA.

Walters, D. L., & Taggart, C. C. (Eds.). (1989). *Readings in music learning theory.* Chicago, IL: GIA.

Weikart, P. S. (2006). *Teaching movement and dance: A sequential approach to rhythmic movement.* Ypsilanti, MI: High/Scope.

INDEX

Page numbers followed by *f* denote figures. Page numbers followed by *t* denote tables.